M000202949

DON'T HONK TWICE

A PRINCE EDWARD COUNTY ANTHOLOGY

Edited by Tanya Finestone & Leigh Nash
Illustrated by Nella Casson

DON'T HONK TWICE

A PRINCE EDWARD COUNTY ANTHOLOGY

Edited by Tanya Finestone & Leigh Nash
Illustrated by Nella Casson

Invisible Publishing

Halifax & Picton

Text copyright © individual contributors, 2019
Introduction copyright © Invisible Publishing, 2019
Illustrations copyright © Nella Casson, 2019

All rights reserved. No part of this publication may be reproduced or trans-
mitted in any form, by any method, without the prior written consent of
the publisher, except by a reviewer, who may use brief excerpts in a review,
or, in the case of photocopying in Canada, a licence from Access Copyright.

Library and Archives Canada Cataloguing in Publication

Title: a Prince Edward County anthology / edited by
    Tanya Finestone & Leigh Nash;
    illustrated by Nella Casson.

Names: Finestone, Tanya, 1969- editor. | Nash, Leigh, 1982- editor. |
Casson, Nella, 1975- illustrator.

Identifiers: Canadiana (print) 20190105356 | Canadiana (ebook)
20190105364 | ISBN 9781988784281
    (softcover) | ISBN 9781988784342 (HTML)

Subjects: LCSH: Prince Edward (Ont.)—Anecdotes.

Classification: LCC FC3095.P75 D66 2019 | DDC 971.3/587—dc23

Cover and interior design by Megan Fildes | Typeset in Laurentian
With thanks to type designer Rod McDonald

Printed and bound in Canada

Invisible Publishing | Halifax & Picton | www.invisiblepublishing.com

We acknowledge the support of the Canada Council for the Arts and
the Ontario Arts Council.

Canada Council
for the Arts

Conseil des Arts
du Canada

ONTARIO ARTS COUNCIL
CONSEIL DES ARTS DE L'ONTARIO
an Ontario government agency
un organisme du gouvernement de l'Ontario

Introduction 1
Belleville 3
City Boy's Luck 4
Stronghold 8
Back in School 15
Sunday at the Bookstore 18
Music in the County 20
Is Ken There? 29
Holy Ground 31
Point Petre Publishing Comes to Life 33
Welcome to the Neighborhood 38
Who Does Your Digging? 40
Bringing Down the Dip 47
Secrets of Main Duck 51
A-frame 55
Lost in Tourist Land 57
Canning Factory Days 59
Moving to the County 61
Helicopters and T-Shirts 65
The Visitor 69
Tree Hugger in the County 72
A Perfect Skate 77
County Journalism 79
Summer Wages at Lakeshore Lodge 85
Treasure at Hallowell Cove 89
The Sweetest Tradition 91
Fire and Frost 101
A Grand Mystery 103
Roughing it in Greenbush 109

Wool Road 114
Coming from Away 119
An Al Purdy Triptych 121
The Meat Roll 123
GWM Looking for Someone to Talk to In PEC 128
Bank Robbery in Wellington 133
From Vinyl Aprons to Tails and White Gloves 134
Just Feels Right 138
Heartbreak Hotel 142
Morley, Written 146
Carving the Vineyard 151
Absinthe on East Lake 155
The One-Man Party 157
County Kindness 160
Full Moon Bay 164
Waupoos Wedding 167
Contributor Biographies 168

INTRODUCTION

This book is equal parts love letter, wayfinder, and snapshot of Prince Edward County. These pages share stories of failure, conflict, growth, and renewal that include and stretch the usual County tropes of farms, wineries, and sand dunes. This isn't just a book of nostalgia, and it definitely does not attempt to pin down a definitive County experience—the whole point is that there is no definitive County experience.

Our hope is that *Don't Honk Twice* will be surprising, elusive, and different. This is a book of County stories, told by the people who lived them. We'd like you to turn to your neighbour and ask them to share their favourite County memory, the one story they always tell over a drink, the rumour or legend they've heard told a thousand different ways.

Our title is a nod to this: it points to a story we couldn't quite pin down. We kept the title anyway, because we feel it is the perfect prompt for you, dear reader, to go out and collect your own anthology of County stories.

Tanya Finestone & Leigh Nash
June 2019

BELLEVILLE

BY DOMENICO CAPILONGO

mouth of the moira
coleman to victoria ave

for lady arabella gore
bay bridge and all

anishinaabe called it
asukhknosk

night before the wedding
friendly drunks on front
f-bomb about the weather

young women share a smoke
outside the bourbon and bean
like a secret handshake

head back to the car
past the empire theatre
in the bay of quinte
i'm reminded
of that al purdy poem

CITY BOY'S LUCK

BY ALAN GRATIAS

The little red tractor was delivered to my property by Anderson Equipment. What's the point of having a farm without the benefit of real traction? When I first moved to Prince Edward County, I had resisted the switch to a half-ton truck, finding that my aging fleet, an Odyssey van with 220,000 kilometres on the second engine and a Honda Element, gave me all the hauling capacity I needed. But a small tractor was a different matter, a necessity because it gave me a loader to dig out slabs of limestone and the power to disk the fields. The therapeutic value for a man to sit on his tractor, moving around payloads of dirt and stone, should not be underestimated. It is as primal as the urge to create shelter.

I didn't go big. Nothing to show off or induce tractor envy. I made a quick decision because I wanted to take advantage of the autumn financing package the manufacturer offered. I liked the understated description of my choice as an "All-purpose compact tractor built for anything you can throw at it. And it still stores in your garage."

In November 2006 I bought a Case DX25E with a loader and cultivator for $19,800. The machine deposited in the courtyard was intimidating—so many levers, knobs, and gears. Since not all men are hardwired to operate heavy equipment, I asked my friend Aubrey to come over for the trial run.

"Break it slowly, hydraulics have a mind of their own," Aubrey advised as I gazed impatiently at the manual. Men are impulsive because they think they know everything. Women tend to make slower and better decisions, but Joanie, my wife, was not on hand to moderate the impulsive moment. A voice kept saying, "Just take it."

"I'm good to go, Aubrey," I called out as I sprang into the cockpit and flipped on the ignition. I raised the shovel, engaged the four wheels, pushed the throttle, and pulled away. Twenty minutes of experimenting with the controls and I was mock cultivating the front field. This is a breeze, I thought: forward, backward, throttle up, throttle down.

My congratulatory monologue was interrupted by an exclamation of phone rings. I rarely answer the telephone, and it would be out of the question on my first spin on the red tractor, but Joanie was gesticulating from the kitchen.

"It's Frank," she called out. "He wants to know when to come over."

Frank Powers, the best farmer in the township, had promised instruction on operating the loader. So confident was I of my skill level that I wanted to move onto the operation of the bucket right away.

"I'll speak to him."

I put the tractor in neutral, cut the engine, and went to the phone. A minute later, my dog Roger was howling at the French doors overlooking the sloped front lawn to the water. The din was more than a plea to be let inside.

"Frank, I'd better go. Roger's in trouble. Come over soon."

I hung up and spun around to deal with my dog. I observed through the window the DXE rolling backward toward the thirty-foot-high escarpment at the water's edge. In the corner of my eye, I caught Aubrey chasing the run-away tractor. I watched, paralyzed, as my $20,000 tractor picked up speed and disappeared over the cliff. I subsequently learned from Frank that you only leave a tractor with its bucket anchored on the ground.

I was flooded with images of my two-hour-old DXE upside down in five feet of water, several of its vital parts floating away. I had not had time to register the Case on my farm insurance policy. "Total writeoff" was the only phrase that came to mind. But when we peered over the cliff, the tractor was not in the water or smashed on the stone beach. By sheer good fortune, the DXE had become lodged in a thicket of protruding Manitoba maples halfway down the cliff face, where it lay like a sailor in a hammock.

Frank came over right away after I sent out the alarm. He drove to the top of the escarpment in his rescue equipment—a full-bore Massey Ferguson 6400 with stabilizers. Frank is also a volunteer firefighter, legendary for his agility in maneuvering the ladders. He operates his twenty-five-foot tractor shovel with the finesse of a painter using a paintbrush. Aubrey, Frank, and I were able to secure a cradle of chains under the machine and link to the extended shovel of the Case.

What a marvel to see this giant steel tentacle hoist its load clear of the cliff, pivot, and land the six-hundred-pound package on the safe terroir of the lawn.

Multiple inspections revealed no water damage, no dents, no missing knobs—not even bruising or chipped paint on the engine cover. The key remained in the ignition.

"Give 'er a go," Aubrey called out. More cautious now, I fixed myself in the saddle and turned the key. The engine purred and I engaged the gears. Aubrey, Frank, and Joanie gawked in amazement as the Case moved forward. Roger started to bark and herd the machine away from the slope.

Aubrey shook his head and muttered to Frank, "That's what I call city boy's luck."

"Just what you need when you move to the County," Frank replied, punching Aubrey in the arm. "It better not run out."

STRONGHOLD

BY ALEX SCHULTZ

I found the body in the wood behind our cabin. The clean curve of its beak caught my eye, something out of place, shining pale in the litter of twigs and rotting maple leaves. Without knowing what it was, I stopped at once. Then the animal, a moment ago a jumble of parts, took shape at my feet. Talons, flight feathers bristling like dark quills, the powerful hook for tearing flesh. A bald eagle, on its back and long dead, its wings fanned out on either side, being slowly subsumed into the ground.

It's a shock to come across an animal's body. Usually it's a quick pang when you pass a raccoon or skunk at the side of the road; sometimes, if you're on foot and the carcass has begun to decompose, it's a stronger jolt mixed with revulsion. But this was different. This was like the body of a beast from some ancient mythology. It was months old, but immediately I found myself trying to imagine what this animal's last hours could have looked like, how long it had hidden there, waiting to die, an alien in our wood so close to where we slept. Had it thrashed about in the brambles and beaten its enormous wings, or hunkered quietly and waited as its last hours wound down, its only movement the stony blink of its inscrutable yellow eye? I could no more imagine a unicorn preparing for death. Suddenly, this wood I'd known for years wasn't so familiar anymore.

When we bought the property on the southeast corner of Waupoos Island, there were no buildings on our sixty-eight acres apart from a wide drive shed and a burned-down barn. There were houses on the island, though. Most of them are late nineteenth-century farmhouses. All of them are summer cottages now; the last year-round residents moved off the island in the 1980s. There even used to be a one-room schoolhouse for the children of families that farmed the land here. And the old cheese factory that served the island community still survives, though it's falling into dilapidation now.

Familiar as they may be to their inhabitants, islands excite the imagination when regarded from a distance. Places apart, tantalizingly out of reach, they hold the possibility of hidden secrets. You look at them from the mainland—in Waupoos, it might be from high up at the Rutherford-Stevens lookout, or from a table laid with lunch on the patio at the County Cider Company—and you can't help but wonder about the mysteries that might be folded into the landscape there. You might think of catching a ride across one day in somebody's boat to explore. Right here, the world seems familiar and unsurprising. Over there, across a kilometre of water, who knows? Someone once swore to me that the Duke of Edinburgh had spent a holiday shooting pheasant on the island. Someone else said that Elton John had come close to buying property there. Neither story is true, but somehow an island makes the unlikely believable.

We gathered up the body of the eagle—its lightness surprised me—packed it in a Coleman cooler, and sent it to the Canadian Co-operative Wildlife Health Centre at the University of Guelph. I wanted to know how it had died, and the pathologists at the centre, who are interested in monitoring bald eagle fatalities, would issue a necropsy report. It's rare to find the body of a mature bald eagle, and because the birds are a species of special concern in this province, it's important to take every opportunity to learn what ultimately kills them.

My biggest worry was that the eagle had been shot. Our neighbours run a big sheep farm on the island, and that spring something had been preying on the newborn lambs. Hunters had come over with hounds to try to flush out a coyote, but the farmer told me that ravens could be the culprits. The lambs had died from puncture wounds to the head; their throats and stomachs had not been torn open, which is what a coyote would do.

What, I thought, if one of the hunters had seen this eagle fly overhead and, deeming it suspect, taken a shot? The idea was sickening. X-rays would tell if this had happened.

For our first two years on Waupoos Island, we were given the use of a stone house on the island's west side as a place to stay. That house is much older than the others. Some say it was built by a fur trader in the 1750s, when this part of Canada was still French. If true, that would make it the oldest house in Ontario.

In the early days, when I looked at the massive two-foot-thick limestone walls of that house and thought about the effort it had taken to dig all that stone from the surrounding land to build it, I found it hard to fathom why anyone would go to so much trouble. Such a substantial dwelling for such an isolated place. Only later did the realization hit me. When this house was built, the island was not the remote place it seems now, cut off from the world by water; it was connected to its surroundings by water. In the days before this land was settled, and in the first decades of farming, there were no roads in these parts. All travel was by the lake. The island was, in fact, a traffic hub on a water highway. It was like suddenly seeing the alternative view in one of those visual tricks in which the negative space magically becomes positive. A different picture, there all along, becomes visible. A white vase becomes two black profiles, nose to nose; a sleepy island becomes a centre of activity. I have thought about the island as an in-between place ever since, where the valence can switch from positive to negative and back again, depending; cut off, yet at the same time more closely connected to an alternative, older, reality.

From our land on Waupoos, we look east across the water to Timber Island, not far from the tip of Prince Edward Point, one of two islands known collectively as the False Ducks. I have read that Timber was the last stronghold of the bald eagle on the Canadian side of Lake Ontario.

In 1917, the amateur ornithologist Edwin Beaupre of Kingston wrote in his journal that the eagles were thought to have occupied "lonely and uninhabited" Timber Island for more than a hundred years. In its day, nearby Waupoos Island would have been home to bald eagles too. But within a few decades of Beaupre's visit to Timber, the eagles were gone, the victims of DDT, a chemical used in agricultural pesticides that weakens the shells of birds' eggs. Bald eagles would still fly through Prince Edward County, and, rarely, maybe stay a while, but no more were to build their massive nests and raise their young here, or anywhere else in Southern Ontario, for a long time.

Slowly, however, the eagles are coming back, and one or two nests have been seen in the County, though no young eagles have yet been successfully raised.

The lawyer in Picton who handled the transfer of title when we bought this land warned us about an oddity concerning the property. Anyone out in a boat on the lake is within their rights to land on our shore if they wish to. I don't know how generally this applies in Prince Edward County or in what legal document it is to be found, but I assume it survives from the days when the lake saw heavy passenger and cargo traffic. Emergencies could develop quickly out on the lake, especially off the County's south shore. This end of Lake Ontario is famous for its unpredictable waters, and the list of wrecks here is long. Severe storms can blow up with little warning, and compasses have been known to go mysteriously awry.

Lakefarers needed to be able to take the shortest route to safety and land on the nearest shore.

Because it's surrounded by water, this place offers a stronger sense of refuge than anywhere I know. In bad weather, if the boat is secure and I don't need to hurry back to the mainland, I become powerfully aware of the island as a place of shelter. As I walk up from the pebble beach, the sound of crashing waves and tumbling stones dies instantly behind me and the land seems to reach up in an embrace. On the rising grass path to the cabin, up past the pond, toward the big ash tree and the row of hawthorns, I become powerfully aware of the solidity of the island, the soil, subsoil, and limestone rock. The island in a storm is eternal, patient, and protective. Walking up the last stretch through the sheep pasture to the cabin is like walking up the back of a huge recumbent beast, ancient and enduring, in a deep, reassuring slumber. You can almost feel it gently stirring just enough to rumble out a low whisper: I've weathered worse. You are safe here.

A few weeks after I sent the bald eagle's body to Guelph, a report came back with some results. The scientists at the wildlife health centre had radiographed the body and run toxicology tests using a long bone from one of the eagle's legs. No broken bones or lead fragments had been found. There was no accumulation of lead in the animal's bones.

Our eagle had not been shot, it had not died from years of slow poisoning, and it had not been fatally injured. It had probably died of natural causes, and I like to think it died of old age. I like to think that, knowing its time was coming, it had drawn on some old inherited memory of familiar, welcoming territory, and chosen our island, our wood, as a quiet place to spend its last hours unobserved. A safe place, secure.

BACK IN SCHOOL

BY ALYSA HAWKINS

I first saw it on Kijiji. My husband and I had been talking about moving out of the city for years, but I was never sure we could do it. We loved our leafy Toronto neighbourhood, and both our parents lived just on the other side of High Park. I had been trolling rural real estate listings for some time but wasn't convinced small-town living could compete with the big city. Still, I kept returning to that one listing: FOR SALE: 10,650 square-foot elementary school in Milford, Prince Edward County.

It looked awful. The outside of the building was painted pastel pink and blue. Inside, there were water stains on the walls from a leaking roof, and rooms filled with musty books and broken bookshelves. It looked abandoned, and a little bit sad.

The size of it was comical. What would our family of five do with so much space? Every crazy idea we could fathom seemed possible in this school. The more we talked about it, the more sane it became. As we pored over the real estate listing, each dusty, chalk-filled crevice was telling us this was where we could begin again and realize our dream of country living.

Most people move back to small towns to be closer to their families, but we would be moving away from ours. My husband and I had lived in Toronto most of our lives. Before we officially met as adults, we were on the same peewee hockey team in Swansea when we were five years old. Our children were in school with the offspring of friends we had known since grade school. Our parents were consistent fixtures in our children's lives. Our community was in west-end Toronto, and frankly, we loved it.

The pull of country living kept resurfacing. We couldn't shake it. We knew no one in Prince Edward County, but that didn't temper our need to leave. The city had become expensive and crowded, and the traffic was unbearable. We craved the space and quiet that only the country could offer.

We moved to the school at the end of June without a kitchen, clean running water, laundry, or heat. I thought we could make do with a BBQ, a cooler, and handwashing our laundry until we got settled, but I panicked on the way to Milford. How were we going to care for, and feed, our three children without the basics? We stopped for an emergency refrigerator purchase on the way, and suddenly, it all felt possible.

In the last year the school was operational, the heating bill had been $38,000. That was neither financially feasible or sustainable. By September, my husband got to work changing our heat from oil to wood pellets. Winter started early in 2013, and it got cold quick. We installed pellet heaters in two classrooms and moved in. It was barely warm enough, and there was no heat in our makeshift kitchen or washroom. Thankfully, we had hot water, so we rigged up a shower in the accessibility stall in the old bathroom. When my kids needed a shower, I would let it run until it was piping hot, bundle them up to walk down our chilly hallway, get them in the water as quickly as I could, then bundle them back up again and sit them in front of the pellet stove to warm up. I was so grateful to send them to a heated school during the day.

We installed a giant wood stove in the gym and bought a large wood pellet boiler from China. A similar boiler bought in North America would have cost $25,000. We gambled and purchased one from Asia for $2,500. My husband had to program it in Mandarin, despite being unilingual. It was up and running for a short period of time, but the Chinese steel consistently broke down due to the high heat in the boiler. At one point, we moved all our beds into the gym around the wood stove to stave off the chilly nights. My husband redesigned the boiler parts and had a local fabricator remake them in Canadian steel. Once we had reliable heat, we knew we could survive our first year in our new home.

Five years in and we are much more comfortable, and grateful to be living in a thriving rural community. Turns out small-town living can compete with the big city, and it may even come out ahead.

SUNDAY AT THE BOOKSTORE

BY ANNE PRESTON

"Good morning, Ella, what a rainy Sunday afternoon. Let's get you something to eat."

After I feed Ella, the bookstore cat, I unlock the doors, turn on the lights, and wait for Mr. Charles to arrive. As surely as ten follows nine, tonic follows gin, Mr. Charles will come in at 10:15 to collect his newspapers, set aside for him during the previous week. Does he read the papers in one gulp or savour them slowly over the upcoming days?

Gradually, the store begins to fill with the Sunday morning crowd. They nurse their lattes, purchased from the adjacent café, peruse the magazines, browse the new releases section, and settle into the comfy chairs in the middle of the store. They are in no rush. An exception to the rule is a rather eccentric couple from Brighton; he quite a bit older, with hair in need of a good wash and cut, and she with a glow in her complexion that says gardening. They do not linger over lattes but head straight to literary criticism, where they spend the better part of the day poring over used books.

Robert arrives. "How's Ella?" he asks. Ella is now dozing in one of the chairs in the children's section. Robert searches for her, always starting on the right side of the store. When he finds her, he spends a few quiet moments, speaking in muted tones as he strokes her black fur. Perhaps they speak of life, how Robert's day is going, the highs and lows of being a bookstore cat. After a while, Robert leaves by walking along the left side of the store.

After lunch, the families arrive and head straight to the children's section in the back corner. Mommies, daddies, sisters, and brothers all curl up in the chairs or sit on the floor—the murmur of stories being read. Nap time approaches and the children are whisked off to their beds. I begin to tidy, placing a copy of *Goodnight Moon* back on the shelf.

"Goodnight books. Goodnight chair. Goodnight noises everywhere."

Sometime in the afternoon, a well-turned-out older couple appear. They have walked the length of the town in order to purchase the Sunday *New York Times*. They are discerning in their taste and I long to be invited to sit in their library, sip tea, and chat about books, art, and life.

During the tourist season, this rhythm is usurped by the allegro, staccato beat as tourists take over the store, flip-flopping over to the mystery and thriller paperbacks, flip-flopping over to the magazines, flip-flopping out the door. Fortunately, summer in Canada is a short season, and the Sunday routine is re-established and righted in short order.

The day draws to a close. I count the till, lock the doors, water and feed Ella. I smile. This is Sunday at the bookstore—a panacea for every woe.

MUSIC IN THE COUNTY

BY ASTRID YOUNG

When I moved to the County in 2002–2003, it was a much different landscape than we see today. As a touring musician, singer and songwriter, I was eager to discover what was going on in the music scene here so I could connect with the community and get involved.

At the time, there were a couple of venues for live music—Alley Cats (where Coach's is now) hosted solo acts and duos doing covers, and the odd singer-songwriter. The Royal was where you'd go to see a band on a Saturday night and dance to top forty until last call. The Waring House was best known for its Celtic, traditional folk, and East Coast flavours. The Legion and the Elks Lodge hosted dances from time to time, often featuring The Reasons (a '50s and '60s cover band that is still going strong to this day), but other than that, you'd pretty much have to go to Belleville to get your live rock fix.

Original music was still pretty underground, but there were a few artists like Emily Fennel, Mark Taylor, Lenni Stewart, Suzanne Pasternak, and Jeanette Arsenault who made regular appearances. Katalin Kiss was easily the biggest ticket in the County, her R&B-tinged brand of blues was always a crowd-pleaser. Any one of these performers on a bill could pretty much guarantee a good turnout with a demographic that ran the gamut from twenty-somethings to seniors and everything in-between.

I made the rounds of those local venues and even played, on occasion, on the patio at the Bean Counter when the mood would strike. Real gigs, however, were few and far between at that time—at least for a solo acoustic act like me.

I had moved to the County from California, where I had spent the better part of three decades recording and touring with various bands. The County, in my estimation, was authentic. It was grassroots. It was a wide-open frontier that hadn't been tapped hard enough to even have a direction, much less a "scene" of its own. That said, any time live music was on offer, it was a big draw and it didn't really matter how accomplished a performer was. From the PEC Jazz Festival to the homespun Music on the Mountain Festival, it was easy to pull an eager crowd. However, it wasn't until the Acoustic Grill came to be that the movement really started to come into focus.

They told him he was crazy. They told him it would never fly. But Steve Purtelle had a vision, and nobody was going to convince him that it couldn't happen. Moved by a dream of having the County's first venue solely dedicated to acoustic music, Steve took over a bar that was originally called Cod Jiggers.

Tucked into an annex of the Elizabeth Building on Main Street, the Cod Jigger was a watering hole with a pool table and local colour galore. It was someplace you usually went to after work for a pint and a game of nine-ball—as I did many a-time, tagging along with my dear friend and neighbour, Grant Howes, owner of the County Cider Company. They kept his cider on tap there, and it wasn't unusual for Grant to buy a round of it for anyone who was in the bar at the time.

But the times were not kind to old Cod Jigger's. Because of their residential neighbours upstairs, they closed up each evening at around seven. Patrons would shift themselves off their barstools and either wander across the street to the Royal to continue drinking or go on home for the night. The streets were generally pretty empty by that time. It wasn't exactly what you'd call "nightlife." A going concern it was not, by any stretch.

When Cod Jiggers was put up for sale in 2005, Steve Purtelle was first in line. As someone who had always dreamed of having a place to nurture his passions—music, beer, and good food—he saw nothing but potential, even though most of his friends and family weren't nearly as optimistic.

He took out the pool table and added more seating. He built a small stage in the corner – plenty big enough for one player, and a cozy situation for a duo. He added an in-house PA system and reimagined the beverage program to include several craft beers (and Grant's cider, of course) on tap. He branded the menu around musical terms. The house burger was "The Acoustic Jam" and the salad was "Composed." The coffee, he admitted, was terrible, but that's not what he was selling. Right from the start, it was all about the music.

The Acoustic Grill may not have been launched to great fanfare, but the roster of musicians that subsequently came through the door was nothing short of awesome. What began with a local focus quickly grew into a destination for serious touring musicians who were travelling through the area, proving that Steve's instinct was good.

The Acoustic was the perfect pick-up gig between Toronto and Kingston or Ottawa, and it brought award-winning artists like Stephen Fearing and Tom Wilson (both of Blackie and the Rodeo Kings), Ken Tizzard (of the Watchmen), Justin Rutledge, Eric Schenkman (Spin Doctors), and John Carroll, to name just a few. Despite the tiny stage, ticketed shows packed people in, and some performers were so popular that it spurred Steve to take his dream to the next level.

Acoustic Jam Records was launched in 2007, focusing exclusively on live recordings of shows at the Acoustic. Their first release was Brock Zeman, and subsequent releases featured Tom Wilson and Ray Farrugia (Junkhouse, Lee Harvey Osmond), Ken Tizzard, Ross Neilson, Tom Savage, Al Lerman, John Carroll, and the Jack Grace Band.

Before long, the Acoustic Grill was firmly established, not only as the premier spot to hear live acoustic music on pretty much any day of the week (Fridays and Saturdays in the off-season, five days a week in the summertime), but also as a destination for Canada's top touring talent, giving our local audiences an opportunity to get up close and personal with Juno-winning artists and up-and-comers alike in a great-sounding, comfortable, and intimate setting.

Lest you think that it's just a County phenomenon, here's a little anecdote that shows just how much Steve Purtelle has done for the music community, both at home and at large. Some years ago, around about 2012, Blackie and the Rodeo Kings were touring the US. They were setting up to play that night in a bar in Chicago, Illinois, when drummer Ray Farrugia (a County resident since 2011) spotted a familiar logo. On closer inspection, there it was—an Acoustic Grill T-shirt.

Turns out, this gentleman, a Chicago native, had been at the Acoustic while Ray had played there some years before with his bandmate in Lee Harvey Osmond, Tom Wilson. Through that experience, he got turned on to Tom's music, and even delved into his previous releases with Junkhouse. That's what brought him to the club that night.

As for the Acoustic, he couldn't say enough about the place. "I wish they had places like that here. I felt right at home."

And that pretty much sums it up. I think I speak for pretty much every musician who has had the pleasure of playing at the Acoustic Grill, past or present: Thanks, Steve. The County's music scene would simply not be what it is today without you.

Today, in stark contrast to what was, County musicians have more venues than ever before. Wineries make good use of them in the warmer months, and there are a dozen or so venues and festivals that feature everything from folk to country, bluegrass, jazz, pop, rock, and even urban music. The Music at Port Milford festival brings world-class classical musicians from all over North America and the annual PEC Jazz Festival is one of the most popular in the province. County Pop and the Sandbanks Music Festival comingle local talent with national acts, and the newly revitalized Hayloft brings in national acts like 54-40 and Sloan.

We also put a significant effort into uplifting young talent here. A partnership between local schools and the ROC, Picton's youth outreach centre, has resulted in a hugely popular annual show, the ROC'N Revue.

Performed at the Regent Theatre, the ROC'N Revue pairs up professional musicians with aspiring young performers in a variety of musical and performance-based disciplines. Each year in May, kids ranging from elementary grades to high school seniors perform their acts to a packed house, each supported by a local mentor who is tasked with coaching and performing with them live on stage. I am proud to say that I have been contributing to this program for the past two years and have had the pleasure of working with some simply amazing young talent. As an artist, I believe that having the opportunity to encourage such expression is a gift, especially in light of the current lack of funding for school music programs.

All of this bodes well for the future of live music in the County. Our local musicians are a busy lot as they all contribute to the local live circuit, which includes wineries, bars, restaurants, small theatres, galleries, house concerts, legions, community centers, and hockey rinks. You can't attend a major event here and not see at least one of them filling the air with sweetness.

It's just what we do.

IS KEN THERE?

BY BECKY MULRIDGE

A person raised in the County will tend to have some unique ingrained traits that they keep wherever they land in life.

I remember being at home and receiving a long-distance phone call, one long ring and two short on the land line. My sister lived in the States so I wasn't overly surprised to be getting a long-distance call, but I was surprised when a man answered my hello.

Is Ken there? he asked.

Umm, no. No Ken here. (This is where the conversation would have normally ended, except it went on.)

Unknown Caller: Shit, I thought this was Kenny's number.

Me: Ha ha sorry, I checked, no Ken here.

Unknown Caller: HA HA okay then. Well who is this? (pause)

Now, I had been living as an adult for about ten years at this point, and as the phone had rung long distance, I wasn't too worried about disclosing my identity to someone who was most likely not within stabbing distance. Still, creepy, right? I think I was shocked into answering honestly.

Me: It's not Ken. Who is *this*?

Unknown Caller: HA HA! Okay, okay, I get it. You are in Picton, right?

Me: Yes. (I mean, he called *me*, so not a huge leap.)

Unknown Caller: You have a Picton phonebook?

Me: (He had me there, and I was catching up.) Yes, I do—can I look up the number for you?

Unknown Caller: Go for it! Kenny Thurston, please and thanks!

So as I looked up the number for him, he let me know Ken was his cousin and it was his birthday and ...

Me: Wait up one minute ... *Ken* is your cousin ...

Not-so-unknown Caller: Yup, Ken's a great guy, I'm calling from BC and—

Me: Robert Biggs?

Robert: YES! Who the hell is this?

Me: Robert, you went to school with my brother and I'm—

Robert: Wait, Jo-Dee, Danyne, or—

Me: It's Becky. Hi Biggsy!

HOLY GROUND

BY BENJAMIN CARTER THORNTON

Full disclosure: I do not now, nor have I ever, lived in Prince Edward County. My mother was born in Picton, married my Torontonian father, and moved away. My grandmother remained, in a little white house on Johnson Street. Growing up, my brothers and I visited her every summer, even after my mother lamentably died when I was three years old.

My childhood memories of the County are my most vivid and would do the local tourism board proud. Sandbanks features prominently, naturally, as do many of the local ice cream establishments that have come and gone over the years. There was an inordinate amount of cheese curd purchased and ingested. With a bit of luck, some social call in Kingston would give us a chance to ride the Glenora ferry.

The centrepiece of every visit to Picton, though, was a stop at Glenwood Cemetery to visit my mother's grave. My father planted sand cherries and roses around her headstone, and our visits became as horticultural as they were commemoratory—a groundskeeper once questioned me closely when he spotted me with a spade over my shoulder. It's a lovely spot, just uphill from where her father and grandparents, old County canners, are buried. My grandmother would some-times come with us when we went, and her bony fingers plucked their share of weeds from around her daughter's stone.

Eventually, of course, my grandmother joined her husband down the hill, after she'd outlived most of her peers whom I knew when I was a child—the neighbour lady who would bake us cookies, for example, or the kindly gentleman with the log home on windswept Huyck's Point. I didn't come to the County as often for a few years, but would still make a yearly pilgrimage with my father and brothers to visit, and tend, the family plots. Once I had children, it became important to introduce them to the family they would never meet. Now, after we've been to the beach or for ice cream, they help with the gardening. And before their own mother died of cancer, she chose the plot next to my mother's in Glenwood. "Holy ground," she called it. "The First Wives' Club," my father calls it.

He was prescient, my father. I am happily remarried after several years of widowerhood, and have a new son, of good United Empire Loyalist stock, who has not yet been to Picton nor yet met the many generations of his family who rest in Glenwood. But, like his brother and sister, he will know he is from Prince Edward County, even if he never lives there.

POINT PETRE PUBLISHING COMES TO LIFE

BY BRIAN L. FLACK

I did *not* come to Prince Edward County to found a publishing company!

Many years ago, in the early 1980s, I attempted to establish a publishing company in Toronto. It was called The Warwick House Press, and it was the end result of a leap of faith I took with another writer. We had the tools: she owned a press; I had skills as an editor. We thought it might work. It didn't. Despite great plans and a fair bit of work, we never got so much as a single title into print. In the wake of this truncated foray, my accomplice continued to write, as did I. And I had my academic career.

At the time, writing and teaching sufficed. But I never forgot how heady our ambition was, and I never stopped thinking about how I might expand my involvement in the world of literary fiction and poetry—as a publisher.

Little did I know that thirty years would pass before I had the opportunity to travel that road again!

Once I settled in PEC, my old itch to be a publisher resurfaced. I decided it might be good for me to bifurcate my life and take another shot. It would be the completion of a circle. I made this decision in 2014, but it was not until 2017 that the first Point Petre Publishing title rolled off the presses.

During those three years, I was part of an attempt that didn't float. It drowned. Nonetheless, I kept thinking about how, on my own, I could both write and run a modest publishing business. I knew I wouldn't be the only publisher in the County, but I knew I could be different. When I finally realized that alone I would not have to twist myself like a pretzel to accommodate a host of ideas not necessarily in line with my own, or accommodate a variety of disparate personalities, I knew I had to forge ahead.

What I wanted to achieve as a publisher could be described as a total artistic accomplishment: important and interesting literature in books that would be readily identifiable as Point Petre Publishing titles. Readers' visual tastes would be rewarded by the design and layout of the books, and their intellectual tastes would be rewarded once they opened a cover and began to read.

Inasmuch as I did not want this "job" to take over my life—I'm not getting any younger and I still have my own books to write—I decided to keep the effort small and regional. Initially, I would try to draw writers from the local population and then, once the effort got some legs, from a hinterland that stretched from the GTA in the west to Ottawa in the east, from the County in the south to Algonquin Park in the north.

I defined this rather compact area because I suspected that the costs of distributing books would weigh against going further afield. They would be unmanageable for a one-man operation publishing only a few books each year. Now, two years down the road, I am certain I was right. So, I will not grow larger than I originally intended. Putting out no more than two books a year, perhaps three in a particularly fruitful year, will test the limits of my work ethic. Along the way, I hope to forge a very personal relationship with everyone I publish, as I work in close collaboration with them to make their work the best it can be.

There are many issues that impede establishing a business in a small rural community, some of which are the sorts of hurdles faced by any business, some of which are unique to publishing. Not the least of those hurdles, for a publisher, is finding, or cultivating, a number of writers. There are plenty of scribblers almost anywhere, but the questions are whether they are publishable, motivated to endure what must be endured to see a book through from conception to "between covers," and prepared to do what must be done, with notable success a long-shot at best. In effect, do they have the vision necessary to work through the difficult, frustrating times in search of that moment when they know everything they did was worth it? Achieving what I want will take time and attention, but it is a laudable goal and if, along the way, I can help a local writer launch him- or herself on the path that leads to wider appreciation, I will consider my job well done!

That said, my idea appears to be working. Writers seem interested. They are not banging on my door in the middle of the night, but they are inquiring and, slowly but surely, forwarding manuscripts. David Sweet's Books & Company has been a great boon, keeping the books I've published in stock, and providing a venue for book launches, at which Brian Mitchell of Half Moon Bay Winery has provided a glass of wine for all who attended. The library has included me in a couple of events—at Loch Sloy and through a local Authors Festival sponsored by the Picton branch itself. I look forward to more. And every book I publish will have a circulating home courtesy of this institution. The Local Store has provided another, albeit seasonal, outlet. The Chapters bookstore in Belleville, and Novel Idea and Indigo in Kingston, have backed my initiative, providing opportunities to have book signing sessions with my authors. Book clubs in the County and in the GTA have invited me to speak to them, and bookstores in both Ottawa and the GTA (and places in between) are beginning to get involved. I have even attended a small press fair in Ottawa, with more to come. Lynn Pickering has given me a great deal of time on her 99.3 FM show *The County Writes ... The County Reads*, as has Vanessa Pandos on 99.3's *Artscene*. Blizzmax Gallery tapped my abilities as a writer, editor, and book designer for its show *Ekphrasis*. And the PEC Arts Council has been there when needed.

Even local non-writers—by that I mean readers—have been very helpful. They have shown their support by attending the launches for Point Petre Publishing titles and buying the books.

For all of this, I am and will remain grateful.

Finally, and this is especially important, I have come to know, through Point Petre Publishing, many County-ites and Quinte-ites I would never have had the pleasure of knowing had I not thrown caution somewhat to the wind and taken the leap—again!

All this is surely a sign that success of any kind starts at home.

WELCOME TO THE NEIGHBOURHOOD

BY BUFFY CARRUTHERS

It was the eighth house we'd looked at in the County. Officially, it wasn't for sale, but the real estate agent was a local, so we got to see it. And the house was a beauty: red brick, Greek Revival and a wreck. One of the oldest in the area. Maybe 1830s.

The farmer had lived in the house all his life. His parents took off, leaving him and his siblings to raise themselves. The last one in the house, he had cows and grew hay on his one hundred acres. But everything was getting old—including him.

We talked in the principal downstairs room. Two wood stoves were going like mad and the farmer stood by one of them, smoking and grinding his cigarette butts into the floor near his cot of tangled, sooty sheets. It was hot. The other downstairs room was cold and empty except for a lump of meat sitting on a table. His refrigerator.

Upstairs, the rooms hadn't been used for years. Fly dirt was piled on the sills. The chimneys were stuffed with ancient straw. But the stairs were generous, with a fine, simple railing.

When we had seen it all, we stood in the driveway to talk it over. The real estate agent pointed to the house across the road. "Do you mind living across from Jimmy Miller?" We looked way across the field at a little house on the other side of the road. Why would we care about Jimmy Miller? By Toronto standards, he was miles away.

When all was agreed and the farmer had been moved to a tiny house in the village, it was ours. We worked for four years cleaning it up, but it didn't take long to get a sense of the neighbour. Most nights, there was a flow of old cars in and out of his driveway. Often, the drivers were so drunk they were practically walking sideways as they carried out their cases of Labatt and Canadian. A thriving bootlegger, Jim had been taking advantage of the short Beer Store hours for years. Never worked, just did a remunerative night shift. A case of beer for double the store price.

One morning, a customer missed Jimmy's driveway and drove into the field west of our house. Looking out the window, we saw a big old Oldsmobile going round and round the field looking for the exit. Finding none, he finally charged the fence. The car came to an abrupt halt, completely encased in fence wire. Then Jimmy ran out of his house, jumped the fence, and hauled the guy out of the car. Shouting and swearing, he drove to the gate with the driver lurching behind.

Jim later declared it was one of the best deals he'd ever made. "The guy gave me a brand-new dishwasher for two cases of beer!"

"But what about our fence?"

"I'll give you a deal on the dishwasher."

And that was the beginning of our life in the County.

WHO DOES YOUR DIGGING?

BY CAROLYN BARNES

Frank and I stood with the young electrician by the road on the muddy edge of our South Bay lot. We all stared down the brambled slope to where the hydro connection would be mounted. "Who does your digging?" the young man asked. "Barry King," we replied, inwardly marvelling that we knew the answer. In the city, where we still lived, the question was never asked. Nobody did our digging there because we didn't have any to do. All the digging in our vicinity was inflicted upon us, by Bell or Toronto Hydro or the City of York, and caused us misery. Here in the County, on the other hand, we dug by choice and with delight. That's because with the digging came the services our beloved piece of land would need before we could make our home on it: the septic tank and tile bed (which is where Barry King first came in), now hydro, and later, when the house went up, the connection to the well.

The well, the first service we installed, didn't actually involve Barry King. It wasn't his kind of digging. In fact, it wasn't digging at all. Ours was a drilled well, bored deep through the limestone that underlies the southern part of the County. Preparations for it began with a visit from George Chalk on a dull fall day in 1990. He was the well driller who, the year before, had drilled the well on the lot next to ours for our friends and future neighbours.

"We had the lot witched before we bought it," we told Mr. Chalk. "The witcher said he found a good place for a well over by that little ash tree. But," we added, "he was our real estate agent's uncle, so he might have felt obliged to find water. And it was raining that day, too, so how could he miss?" We shared a chuckle over these water-dowsing pleasantries, and then Mr. Chalk got to work.

He walked slowly over the property, arms outstretched, gripping the sturdy forked stick he'd brought with him. "You can use wood from any fruit tree as long as the fruit has a stone in it," he told us. From time to time, the stick arced down, seemingly of its own accord, until the end pointed straight down at the ground. Whenever that happened, Mr. Chalk stepped back a few paces, walked around the place where the stick pointed, and approached it again from a different direction. The stick always started out in a horizontal position and always ended up pointing down at the spot.

When he finished traversing the lot, he told us he'd found water in a few places, including the one the agent's uncle had noted, but recommended a different location with an even stronger flow. "Would you like to try?" he asked. To our disappointment, the forked stick didn't budge for either one of us, no matter where we carried it. Then we picked up the bent wires, one in each hand, which in the grip of a dowser swing toward one another and stay crossed above a likely place. Unlike the stick, the wires worked for us—too well. When I passed over Mr. Chalk's chosen location, the wire I held in my right hand whipped around so fast and so forcefully that it whacked me on the face and scratched my cheek. It hurt a lot, and I was lucky it had missed my eye, but I took this assault as a good sign. "I'll drill in the spring," Mr. Chalk said.

Many months later, after the snow had melted, we got a call at home from the friends who owned the lot next to ours. They lived in Toronto too, but they'd gone to the County for a few days to check on their property. "There's a drill rig set up on your land," our future neighbour told us. "They're down sixty feet already and haven't found a thing. How much did you say you're paying a foot?"

Eventually, at ninety-six feet, Mr. Chalk found water. Sulphurous, but most of the wells in our neighbourhood are sulphurous. An aerator would easily get rid of the sulphur and we had a good flow, just as the witching had predicted. Enough to run our future County household three or four times over.

The year after the well went in, we had the septic tank and tile bed installed. As with the well, we simply contacted the contractor our neighbours had hired, in this case Bob Wood. The three of us—Frank, Bob, and I—stood together at the edge of the lot. "Where is your house going to go?" he asked. A few more questions about the size of the house and the number of bathrooms, a bit of pleasant chitchat, and we went our separate ways.

With Barry King's help on the digging, Bob installed the tank and bed a few weeks later. We found out later that, after the job was done, he had to ask another neighbour who we actually were so he could put names on the invoice and the permits. Until that point, it had been good enough for him that we were Frank and Carolyn, friends of the people whose system he'd installed the year before. It probably didn't hurt that we were also friendly with the antique dealer who lived down the road, a fellow he'd gone to school with, who called him Bobby. Those were sufficient credentials in the County, even for a substantial job.

When it came time to build the house, we encountered another example of the trust that can bolster professional relationships in the County. We designed the house and detailed the specifications ourselves, and Frank did the drawings. As with the other projects, we chose the contractor, Elmer Terpstra, our friends had used to build their house the year before. We met with Elmer and his son, Roy, several times over the winter of 1993–1994 to finalize the plans. Elmer informally quoted a price that was satisfactory to both parties. Thinking like Torontonians, we figured it would be a good idea to have something more official. A friend at work who had practised real estate law in a previous life helped me draw up a simple, solid contract that incorporated everything we had agreed upon with Elmer. When I handed the document to Elmer, he didn't even look at it. He signed it quickly and handed it back to me. I sensed that, kindly and gently, we were being taught a lesson.

We were city people and didn't fully understand how the County worked, but as we prepared the land

and built the house, we learned. About trust. About an ancient skill that borders on the magical. About how neighbourly connections are valued. And we learned that the County had turned us into people who are asked "Who does your digging?" and who know the answer.

BRINGING DOWN THE DIP

BY J.D. CARPENTER

In 1980, my brother and his wife bought an old farm-house on Salmon Point. My family and I were frequent guests, and my children spent many hours playing with their cousins and swimming off the limestone ledges of Athol Bay. In 1983, I asked my brother if I could put a cabin in the maple grove halfway down to the water. He talked it over with his wife, and they said I could.

I discovered that a log cabin was beyond my budget, so instead I purchased a former Dari-Dip building that was up on beams near Colton's Meadow, on East Lake Road. It was twenty-four feet by thirty-two feet, had no floor, just walls and windows—including a big picture window and two sliding serving windows—and a good roof. I paid two thousand dollars for it.

I hired a mason to make a concrete pad for the Dip. When it was finished, all I had to do was move the building eight miles to my brother's. So I phoned a house-moving company in Belleville. A man answered, and I explained my situation.

"No problem," he said.

"How much?" I asked.

"Three grand."

"But that's more than I paid for the building."

"Then it probably ain't worth movin'."

I looked around some more and found a local man,

Russell Cole, who said he could do the job for three hundred dollars. "Great!" I said, and hired him. He arrived at Colton's Meadow on the appointed day with a homemade flatbed trailer pulled by an industrial-strength tow truck. He was tall and raw-boned and wore a Pickseed cap and a Mickey Mouse muscle shirt. He had a young man with him—his daughter's boyfriend, as I recall—and a runaway kid he'd found at the pool hall in Picton and taken in.

Russell backed his trailer under the Dari-Dip, then used about a dozen truck jacks to lift the building off its beams. He removed the beams, lowered the Dip onto the trailer, and transported it—with a police escort, no less—to Salmon Point. My brother filmed the whole thing, including the moment when a section of wall fell off. Russell backed the trailer halfway down the hill toward Athol Bay and onto the concrete pad where, again using the truck jacks, he raised the Dip off the trailer. He pulled the trailer out and walked around the Dip, stopping at each jack and lowering it a notch at a time with a crowbar until the Dip was four inches above the pad. At this point, he placed an iron pipe—about two feet long—under each corner of the building and lowered it the rest of the way so that each corner was resting on a pipe. He said, "Is she pointed at the lake just right?"

I looked at the Dip and I looked at the bay and I said, "Actually, it would be better if it was facing a little more to the left."

He got down on his knees near one corner, slid the crowbar into the pipe, said, "Tell me when to stop," leaned his shoulder against the wall, and swung the building on its rollers.

"Whoa!" I said.

He got back on his feet and knocked the pipes out with a sledgehammer.

Sometime later, I was talking to Ralph Quaiff, who farmed down the road from my brother, and I told him about Russell moving the Dari-Dip, and Ralph said, "Oh, Russell's pretty good at that kind of thing, but he loses houses. One time, he lost a brick house off Gommorah Road into a cornfield. Sheared off a hydro pole one time over at Woodrous. 'Nother time, a fella ordered a bunch of septic tanks for a campground, but never paid for 'em. He had 'em stacked inside one of those domes—like the domes the roads department uses to store sand and salt. The bank or whoever the fella owed the money to hired Russell to repossess the tanks, so Russell brought his trailer out to the fella's property, and the fella slid the door of the dome open and Russell drove inside and used his winch to load up the tanks. But then the fella musta changed his mind 'cause he closed the door and locked Russell inside. So Russell, being a good ol' County boy, put his gearshift in low and drove straight through the wall."

When all was said and done, the Dari-Dip didn't turn out to be the perfect little cabin I'd hoped for. It was fine at first: the day we moved in, my brother ran extension cords down from his house and strung Christmas lights all around the Dip, and we served champagne and ice cream through the serving windows to the neighbours. But a million spiders moved in too, and it was so damp that large white fungi grew through the blue shag carpet I'd laid, and my kids refused to sleep in it.

In 1988, I bought thirty-six acres on the Walmsley Crossroad and put a house trailer in the geographic centre and more or less forgot about the Dip. Time passed, and I was happily ensconced on my land when my brother called me one spring morning and said, "You're not using the Dip anymore, and it's become an eyesore. Kindly get rid of it."

So, ten years after Russell Cole installed the Dip, I hired him to remove it. When I asked how much it would cost, he said, "How much did you pay me to put it there in the first place?"

"Three hundred dollars."

"Well then, how's three twenty-five?"

On the appointed day, he arrived with his tow truck and trailer and got to work. But as he lifted the Dip with the truck jacks it started to fall in on itself, so he demolished it with his sledgehammer, loaded the remains on the trailer, and hauled it all away.

A few months later, I bumped into him at Giant Tiger. "What did you ever do with that Dari-Dip?" I asked him.

"Oh, that," he said. "Took it out to the back forty and burned it."

Note: "Bringing Down the Dip" originally appeared as a poem in *County Magazine* #73 (Fall, 1994).

SECRETS OF MAIN DUCK

BY CHERYL BRUCE

My grandfather, Adrian, was born on Boxing Day of 1916, in a house nestled deep in the heart of South Bay. Times were tough, the weather was cold, and the doctor didn't think he would live, but he defied the odds for more than ninety years. He was a Dulmage, of solid Prince Edward County Loyalist stock; a family of men who were tied to the water, both by profession and predilection; of lighthouse-keepers and fishermen.

As a child, Adrian lived in Picton during the winter, but his summers were spent in paradise. His father, Milt, was a commercial fisherman on Main Duck, a small island roughly halfway between Point Traverse in Prince Edward County and Sacket's Harbor in New York state, and the family stayed in residence there from May to October.

Adrian occupied his time exploring the island. The water held all kinds of wonders, and it was there that he learned to swim, splashing over the remains of a ship that had floundered off Schoolhouse Bay. Inland was no less exciting: the owner of the island at the time, C.W. (known as King) Cole had a farm where he raised buffalo, along with more traditional animals. One summer he even kept a grizzly bear chained by the shore.

My grandfather told me many stories about Main Duck Island, and his love for the place was abundantly evident. He made his time there sound idealistic, but the island is infamous for activities more nefarious than commercial fishing: it acted as a stopover for rum-runners carrying their bootleg alcohol to the United States during Prohibition, and Adrian was there for that too.

Fishing boats were the perfect cover for illicit activities, and some of the fishermen did double duty. Though they plied their illegal trade by the cover of night, Adrian knew many of the men by day. His favourite story to tell about the island involved some of their precious cargo.

Adrian's mother, Leah, was a teetotaler and supporter of the Temperance movement; clearly, she did not approve of the bootlegging activities that pervaded the island. One day, she and Adrian came across some burlap sacks when they were walking along the shoreline. There was no doubt about their contents, as the brown necks of beer bottles poked over the edges.

No one else was around—one of the fishermen must have unloaded his nightly stash in preparation for a later run. Leah hatched a plan: she and Adrian would bury the bottles in the sand, silently demonstrating her disapproval and thwarting the bootleggers in their trade. In Adrian's mind, though, this would be a great adventure, akin to discovering pirate treasure and claiming it for his own. The two of them got to work, and soon the bottles were out of sight.

I imagine an exciting end to the tale—one of angry rum-runners tearing up the shoreline to find the lost cargo, or a treasure hunter coming across priceless Prohibition-era bottles decades later.

Unfortunately, my grandfather never knew for certain what happened to the missing bottles. What I do know is that we returned to Main Duck together in 1995. He showed me the cement step that once led to his cottage, and the stone chimney that is all that remains of John Foster Dulles' home—the future U.S. Secretary of State who lived there in 1941. But, though we searched the beach, the beer bottles were nowhere to be found.

What we think most likely happened is that Leah told her husband about the day's activities and he returned the goods; Milt did, after all, have to work with those men for half of the year. But it's more fun to think that there might be century-old bottles still buried somewhere on the island, lost in time. All we need is a treasure map to find them.

A-FRAME

BY CHRISTIAN WEBBER

The A-frame is where K and I broke up—one of the times we broke up. It was the first place we visited together; we took the bus from Toronto and Katherine picked us up at the station.

I was really into taking prescription painkillers along with my SSRIs. I wasn't drinking or smoking at the time, but sure did love those little white pills, and when they weren't around, the blue ones.

K and I had been together for a couple of months maybe, and had broken up a few times already. It's hard to say how long we were really together. It's hard to even think of how terrible a match we were. Somehow, someone up there was teaching us both a valuable lesson, one I'm grateful to have learned.

Katherine was staying at Al Purdy's A-frame because she was a poet and had won a summer residency as a prize. She was there alone and wanted her roommate—K—to come visit, along with some other friends. K was in love with PEC: the wineries, the farmland, the lakes, the sandbanks, the stores. The potential.

We broke up because she was too afraid to use the ladder to come down from the loft of the A-frame. I may or may not have lost my temper trying to coax her down. I guess we made up, because we went on to break up several more times, both inside PEC and out.

We walked the lanes between farmers' fields in the morning, and lay by the lake in the afternoon. We played on the dunes at Sandbanks. We both liked to take pictures, and she liked to have her picture taken. It was special to me to be at Al Purdy's place, even though I didn't know who he was yet. He was a writer, and so was I.

I fell in love with PEC as I'm sure most people who visit there do. I thought I fell in love with K there, too, writing it slowly on her back as she napped in my lap on the bus ride home, spelling it out in all caps: I L O V E Y O U.

LOST IN TOURIST LAND

BY CHRISTINE RENAUD

I'm out on a limb here. Maybe it would be safer to write about the heady scent of lilacs in May, or the magnificent sunsets. Or I could tell you of the deer that visit our field, illuminated like ghosts by a full moon. Or about the times my husband and our kids marked autumnal equinox on the shores of Point Petre, sharing roasted potatoes and sipping hot chocolate from Thermoses as we waited for the darkening lake to swallow its tangerine sun. And I could—and feel I must—also tell you of the people that I've come to know and deeply love here in the twenty years that I have called the County home. Soul-nourishing relationships, familiar faces on the street, memories of friends' children growing up, including my own, ground me here. These days, I could easily go on as well about artisanal cheese, charcuterie, craft beer, pinot noir, vintage markets, and boutique hotels, though you can learn about those in the glossy brochures that grow anew in abundance each spring like roadside weeds.

What I cannot tell you, however, is where to find the brochure that reveals the insatiable hunger for tourism dollars that has created a crippling lack of affordable housing, or efforts to entice youth to the hospitality industry to build a steady pool of workers for the low-paying, precarious seasonal job market, or about the migrant workers who picked the grapes for that pinot.

I'm often tempted to design my own brochure inspired by street art I saw recently that read "Gentrification in Progress. There will be cupcakes!"

Ruth Glass, the sociologist who coined the word gentrification, wrote, "Once this process of gentrification starts in a district it goes on rapidly until all or most of the original working-class occupiers are displaced and the whole social character of the district is changed." And changed we are, while the economic interests of investors and business are well-served, and restaurants and shops increasingly cater to the tastes of a growing demographic of hip and well-off clientele.

Gentrification has also added to the underlying tension I felt only mildly twenty years ago between the County folks and newcomers. Today, despite what one might think with an influx of progressives—even lefties—those conversations are increasingly awkward, unless, of course, I'm with those on the losing end of the increasing gap between rich and poor.

Agitating to change the direction in which we're headed is water on the fire of capitalist accumulation. A stick in the wheels of profit. Rejecting the lure of entrepreneurship, luxury living, and limousines can make one mighty unpopular.

Some brand me a dreamer to believe it could be different. Trust me, I am not. Dreamers are those who think we can continue on the unjust and unsustainable path we're on. No, I'm just a lover of the County, out on a limb.

CANNING FACTORY DAYS

BY DEBBIE HYATT

It's June 1966, and I am twelve years old. S.S. No. 13 Hallowell, the two-room school house that I attend, has been let out for the summer. The long-anticipated time for my family and me to move from our neat, white bungalow on the west side of West Lake to our sagging, grass-green cottage on the Cherry Valley side of East Lake has finally come.

Our cottage is located behind my family's canning factory, and we will hunker down here for the next two months. The large windows that swing up and hook to the ceilings are mostly always open to allow in the breeze. It carries the funky, unmistakable smell of the marshy shoreline we perch on. We live close to the earth, and the couch I curl up to read on, and the old bed I sleep in, always feel slightly damp.

We are here for the summer to make it easier for Dad to work the long hours required at the factory when the peas (and then the raspberries, and then the tomatoes) are ready to go "into the can." So, off he goes first thing in the morning—crossing our shaggy little front yard and then the boiler room cinder yard. It isn't long before I follow him into what is for him a place of work, and what is for me a place of comfort and fascination.

I feel at home in the factory because I belong here. The majority of the people who work here return each summer to perform the same jobs year after year. It may be an overstatement to say we are an extended family, but that's how it feels. This often leads to some good-natured teasing, and to me pattering up the factory lane in bare feet to Bell's store where—*can you believe it?*—a live spider monkey peers at me from behind the counter with beady, mischievous eyes as I buy Earl's cigarettes. The change is mine to keep, and later I will buy a toppling soft ice cream cone further up the Cherry Valley road at Leavitt's dairy bar.

I know every square inch of the factory and every step in the fascinating, transformational process that turns raw produce into a finished product. The produce, brought in by trucks from the local farmers' fields, is sealed in cans that are then labelled, boxed, and eventually hauled out to grocery stores by transports. And not only do I know the people responsible for this magic, but I also know the machines they operate—each with its own clamorous sound, its own danger, and its own quirky temperament.

I don't realize it at the time, but these canning factory days in Prince Edward County will soon be just one more thing of the past left to be remembered by those of us who lived them.

MOVING TO THE COUNTY

BY DEBORAH TROOP

"Have you ever heard of Prince Edward County?" asked my real estate friend.

"No," I answered. "Where is it?"

"You've heard of Picton?"

"I think so," I mumbled." Where's that again?"

"It's the capital of Prince Edward County!"

"Oh," I was starting to feel foolish. "What's so remarkable about Prince Edward County?"

"It's by the great lake, Ontario."

"Okay, that sounds interesting."

I was looking to return to Canada after being away in Ireland for over fifty years. A place near water, as I was used to being not far from the sea.

"You could go online and look at the houses for sale," my friend told me. We did, and both of us fell in love with an old brick house in a place called Bloomfield, which I understood was in Prince Edward County.

Padraig, my partner of nearly thirty years, had been made redundant over the 2008 recession, and getting another job seemed unlikely. Then his mother died, unexpectedly leaving him a lot of money. She had been playing the stock market for years and had not told her son about it. We decided to use our newfound wealth and move to Canada. It was to be our last great adventure, because I was in my seventies and Padraig had hepatitis C. However, the doctors in Dublin had given him the all clear when they heard that he was emigrating to Canada.

We got in touch with a County real estate agent and flew over. We arrived in Picton on a Wednesday. It was October and the leaves were glorious in their vibrant colours. We had come to see the house in Bloomfield, and see it we did on the Thursday. We were enchanted. We viewed it again on Friday and made an offer. Saturday, we bought it! We left on Sunday. Both of us were terrified at the enormity of what we had done! This was 2010. We moved here lock, stock, and barrel, including a dog and two cats, a year later.

We were astonished at the generosity of our new County friends. They offered us a house to live in until our furniture arrived by sea from Ireland. It was a real godsend because we had a difficult time at the Toronto airport. We couldn't find our pets. No one knew where they were. I felt like an ewe crying out for her lambs. Luckily, I had the foresight to book a driver to meet us with his large truck. He, being a County man, couldn't have been more patient, and hung in there until all was well and we had our three pets on board. He got us safely to Picton. Everywhere we went with our dog, we were greeted with enthusiasm and interest about where we had come from. I was astounded by the friendliness of County people.

Two weeks later, the day our furniture arrived, there was a huge thunderstorm—a portent of things to come. We settled into our house in Bloomfield and so did our animals. The cats were delighted with the variety of creatures they could catch, especially snakes, since there are no snakes in Ireland. Our neighbours across the road became good friends almost on sight and have remained so ever since.

I was a Canadian by birth, and the plan was for me to sponsor Padraig into becoming a Canadian citizen. Everyone once again was helpful and gave us the right information on how this could be done. We decided it would be a good idea to get married to speed up Padraig's permanent residency. So, within two months of arriving in the County, we were married in our beautiful new home in Bloomfield. It was December 2011. We had gotten to know enough County people that we had about forty guests. A few friends came from Toronto as well. Even though we had come from so far away, we were accepted by the County. It was a grand occasion. We felt jubilant and truly blessed. (It was my third wedding!)

As I mentioned, Padraig had hepatitis C. Sadly, about three months into the next year, Padraig became very ill. He died just a year after we moved here. It was a terrible time, but I managed to survive because of the infinite kindness of my County friends. I am now hale and hearty and thriving, all due to the magic of Prince Edward County.

HELICOPTERS AND T-SHIRTS

BY GABY COLE based on events shared by
her father, Timothy Martin Cole

The most striking memories I have of the County were created by the scathingly brilliant ideas and humorous antics of my father. Growing up in a small town was often financially difficult and isolating, but it resulted in stories that, decades later, I still use to define myself and how I fit into this community.

For a short time in the 1990s, my father filled the tiny hamlet of Bloomfield with the sweet smell of burning applewood on Saturday mornings. Getting up early, he would burn the wood in a cylindrical BBQ in the parking lot behind our convenience store and pizza shop. The coals were then taken to the front of the building in a wheelbarrow and, throughout the day, he slowly cooked chickens in a large black rotisserie right on Main Street.

When something unusual happens in a small town, it rarely goes unnoticed. The first indication that something peculiar was happening in our tiny village was the appearance of an unmarked police vehicle in the parking lot. The car sat there for weeks. Then, there was a curious baseball game in the park. Our house was on the end of Brick Street, right before the mill pond. The park that skirts the pond had a poorly kept and rarely used baseball diamond. One afternoon, a group of men was spotted playing on the diamond; they were strangers in dress shirts and ties.

Not long after that, the news broke. In July 1997, it was revealed that thirty-four US army helicopters were being stored in the old Baxter Canning factory on Stanley Street. A sting operation by Canadian authorities and police in Florida had foiled a private plot to sell the Vietnam-era choppers to Iraq.

Dad sprang immediately into action. He had been creating custom T-shirts and sweatshirts for over a decade to commemorate special occasions and local characters. Working with local artist Johnny Miller, he laid out what he envisioned. He had statistics and quips, characters and spies, all to be woven into a design starring our Bloomfield pizza shop, Luigi's, and the newly established Slickers homemade ice cream parlour. Even the rotisserie was featured.

The T-shirt's design was part of a bigger backstory for us. Stylistically, it derived from a comic strip featured in the *Picton Gazette* advertising the newly opened Rock & Roll Luigi's Pizza, our second pizza place, which we ran in Picton. The comic starred Elvis—who was not dead but living in the County and growing fatter on Dad's pizza—and Luigi himself, a persona my dad took on for the shop based on a nickname given to him by a patron. The comic featured satirical takes on Luigi's interventions in famous musical moments and local events, such as the installation of the stoplights around Tim Horton's. This new T-shirt placed Luigi right in the scandal, piloting a helicopter with Elvis as his co-pilot, flying over our shop. The tagline read: "Bloomfield. World's most over-protected village, 1 attack chopper per 19.6 people!!!"

Miller drew the idea in less than a day, allowing Dad to get the image to a Trenton printing company. The printers worked through the night and, by morning, T-shirts were stacked and ready for the circus that was about to unfold.

News crews swarmed the town. Unable to get into Baxter's, they were redirected by the RCMP to a small mom-and-pop convenience store up the street where Dad's T-shirts were already available for sale. News channels were quick to pick up the story of the shirts and they were featured in local and national papers. We are told we even had a spot on the Royal Canadian Air Farce, whose name Dad had borrowed for part of the design. Tourists and locals alike—even members of the RCMP and FBI—stopped in to buy them and send them all over the world. The shirts were a hit!

When time came for the annual Christmas parade, the community had to celebrate its newfound notoriety. Santa would not drive a sleigh that year. Unsatisfied with our rate of one attack helicopter per 19.6 people, one Bloomfield resident had a chopper of the same make and model that he kept on his property. This was set up on a flatbed truck and decorated with lights for the town's night parade. There was only one person who could play Santa: settling into the helicopter, my dad took absolute delight in being surrounded by a dashboard with buttons to launch rockets and triggers to shoot machine guns. That Christmas, Santa launched a full imaginary attack on the unsuspecting residents of Bloomfield.

When something extraordinary happens in a small town, it is rarely forgotten. The story of the day the RCMP descended on our sleepy, occasionally smoky, town is shared regularly between locals and joked about at gatherings. July 2017 marked the twentieth anniversary of the "Bloomfield Air Farce." *County Magazine* featured the T-shirt design in their Spring 2018 issue and every so often it pops up on social media with wistful commentary.

For me, it is a small part of County lore that my dad carved out for us and I am proud that this story is part of the wild history of Prince Edward County.

THE VISITOR

BY GERRY JENKISON

Wild turkeys pass through our south field quite often, though they don't often come anywhere near our farmhouse. But looking through the bedroom window on a late September morning, I saw a huge male in full display on the other side of our garden fence.

We'd been raising Ridley Bronze turkeys for several years at our farm in Hillier. They are Canada's only heritage turkey, developed in Saskatchewan almost a hundred years ago, and, until recently, they were considered a rare breed. Had it not been for a last-minute intervention by Rare Breeds Canada, they would have died out.

"If you like chickens, you'll love turkeys," our supplier told us. He was right. Turkeys are curious and socialize well with people. We kept them free-range and they often followed us around the farm. Once, when my husband was repairing the fence, they formed a semi-circle around him and watched the whole time. They hung around the back door, waiting for us to come out. We kept two, and would have kept more if our shed was bigger. We named them Lucy and Tomas.

So when the wild turkey showed up, I figured he'd sussed out Lucy. He'd come to impress her, and impressive he was. In most ways, he looked like Tomas, except taller. He was elegant. His bronze feathers shone in the sun. His wattle was the colour of a pale sky at dawn, and his tail feathers made an enormous fan. Judging from the length of his beard—male turkeys have a black, bristly tassel hanging from their chest—I figured he was at least five years old. I ran downstairs for a closer look, hoping he'd stick around.

And he did. Stood stock still for what seemed like a long time before sauntering into the garden and almost to the house. I joined Tomas and Lucy on the porch, anxious but fascinated.

Tomas, also in full display, left the porch to engage him. Male turkeys fight viciously. They jump off the ground and meet in mid-air, trying to slash each other with their long, sharp spurs. I wasn't confident of Tomas's chances, seeing that he was smaller, heavier, and not exactly battle-hardened.

To my surprise, it was a short fight—no more than a minute or two—with no blood spilled. The visitor withdrew elegantly. Why so soon? Had he made his point—I wondered if it was to let Lucy get a good look at him?

Withdrawing involved a slow and dignified walk back the way he'd come, still displaying his finery. He stopped again at the outer fence, looked back at us, and then continued into the woods.

Tomas hopped on the fence, a good vantage point, then flew down to track the visitor for a while, making sure he'd really gone.

And Lucy? She seemed nonchalant, but later that afternoon I noticed her walking down the road to the south field. She didn't come back till around ten the next morning, her feathers unkempt from a night's rollicking.

We see wild turkeys running through our fields from time to time. We raised heritage turkeys for several more years after this adventure of Lucy's. She died two years ago, and we still miss her. Tomas is still with us. His best friends now are two of our egg chickens— Wanda and Rhonda.

TREE HUGGER IN THE COUNTY

BY HELEN WILLIAMS

1.

Considering each plant in our yard, I discovered most arrived with a story. A young mountain-ash near the driveway between our house and barn has a history all its own.

Years ago, a row of Manitoba and hard maples formed a boundary line in front of our property. When planted at the beginning of the nineteenth century, horse-drawn vehicles travelled the nearby dirt road. Year by year, these poor trees succumbed to age and unrelenting collisions with the speeding vehicles that missed the sharp curve. Finally, only one remained.

During its last years, a robin, having a picnic of round red mountain-ash berries, dropped a seed in the decaying crevice. Rains fell, sun beat down, and frost broke down the old wood mixed with dust from the road. Gradually, a tiny plant sent down roots into the mixture.

The mother tree soon gave up. It lost its life limb by limb, but the little adopted baby grew tall in its comforting cradle.

In February 2001, Bill, a kind woodsman, was hired to do controlled lumbering in our woods on the farm. We asked him to cut our beloved old maple. He would skid it over the icy road in front of our house to join the pile of other logs on our dairy farm.

"I have to go to town. I don't want to see that tree being cut," I informed my husband Bob. But I had neglected to tell him my plan. Upon returning, the log was nowhere in sight. "Where did that baby go? I have to find it."

Winter winds blew and piled the snow high as I searched for the special log among the stack behind the implement shed. "There it is."

2.

Through many years, my husband Bob has grown to not be so shocked by my unusual ideas, but poor Bill. He was from Madoc, where mountain-ashes are weed trees.

Carefully, the rotting section containing the baby was cut and tractored back to our barnyard. Spring arrived, geese flew north, daffodils sprung up around the other trees in our yard. Chipping away the rotted wood to expose the mat of roots, we covered it with wet burlap.

Near the stump of the momma maple, a large hole was dug. We spread the roots, added mulch, pounded in steel stakes for protection, and then waited while spring rains settled it in its new home.

A crash summoned us to the yard. A half-ton truck with too much speed or a driver with too much liquor had missed the curve and headed straight for our little tree, bending the stakes and skinning the plant badly. "I'm so sorry," choked the driver, just as I was ready to choke him.

We weren't giving up. With my trusty Swiss Army knife, I trimmed the wound and administered a rubbing alcohol solution with a small brush.

Our tree is now a teenager, about thirty feet tall and covered in the fall with a multitude of scarlet berries. Mother Nature healed the wound enough for it to survive. Robins and cedar waxwings devour the fruit.

I wonder if Bill, our woodsman, remembers when he kindly helped to rescue a tiny mountain-ash from a pile of logs headed for a lumber or pulp mill. He is likely happy he doesn't have to face tree huggers every day in his job.

A PERFECT SKATE

BY HILARY ARTHUR AMOLINS

I was sitting on my dock on Consecon Lake, enjoying a frosty beer on a sunlit January day. The year escapes me, but it was a brilliant winter, lots of sunshine, and the ice was a mirror sheet reflecting the sun's rays in all directions. Snow had not yet fallen on the frozen surface, so I had my skates with me and was looking forward to going out for a spin. It is rare to see such perfect conditions on Consecon Lake and we had learned through the years to seize the skating opportunities when no shovelling of snow was required. You could skate the length and breadth of the lake, going quite literally for miles and miles.

Ice fishermen had parked their huts around their favourite spots. Several were grouped together at the western end near the old railroad bridge. I had already drilled a couple of holes to determine thickness and the presence of the huts confirmed the ice was quite safe.

I noticed a shape moving east, from the general vicinity of the ice huts. At first I thought it might be an ice boat taking advantage of the glaze conditions and the developing wind. Our prevailing winds come from the southwest, and as they picked up in speed, it became apparent what I was observing. One of the ice huts was slowly pirouetting its way down the lake! It was a jaw-dropping moment. An old-school ice hut, made from wood, a little bit larger than an outhouse.

In fact, with the door and slope roof, that's exactly what it looked like! The wind encouraged it forward. I had to shake my head and blink my eyes to confirm this vision, yet there it was, fast approaching our end of the lake. It gained speed as it drew near, the slow revolutions accelerating. If a Mozart waltz had been playing in the background, it would have made for a perfect Monty Python skit.

Dumbfounded as it passed in front of me, I estimated its speed at a solid twenty-five miles per hour, still upright and still spinning. I watched it head east until it eventually hit a pressure crack and tumbled on its side. And there it sat for a couple of days, until its owner showed up with an ATV and towed it back to its brothers and sisters by the bridge. Had I not been sitting there, witness to this extraordinary sight and instead heard this story from another, I would have chalked it up to a good old County yarn. But I can swear on the King James that it happened: I witnessed the skating ice hut of Consecon Lake.

COUNTY JOURNALISM

BY JACK EVANS

After sixty years as a journalist in communities across Ontario, I still think often and fondly of my years in Picton. I arrived in the fall of 1963 as bureau chief for the *Kingston Whig-Standard*. Picton was one of three bureau points for the *Whig* at that time, in addition to the main office. The other two were at Gananoque and Napanee. The bureaus and their copy were managed by a district editor. We communicated and filed stories by teletype. Rolls of film were delivered to Kingston via courier.

It was a time when the late Harvey J. McFarland, millionaire construction tycoon and hockey team sponsor, was firmly entrenched as mayor. In fact, my editor made it clear that the *Whig* was highly suspicious of the small-town tycoon and urged me to dig up any dirt I could find. I soon arranged an interview with McFarland and learned the suspicion was mutual. He accused the paper of distorted journalism. I told him: "I am a newsman. I'm here to cover the news in Prince Edward County ... both the good news and the bad news. I am not out to get you, or anybody else." He seemed to accept my pledge and we got along fine for years until his death, at which time I was a member of his town council and served as an honourary pallbearer. He was certainly a colourful character, prone to losing his temper in heated political arguments.

McFarland also loved machinery. On an outing to a steam equipment exhibition in Milton one year, he jumped on the back of a panting steamroller and quickly showed he knew how to use it. He also told me his life story. As a teenager, he had a chance to get a good-paying contract to haul lumber out of a wood. He sought a loan from the local bank manager, who knew him and his family. He had to turn down the request because his father could not back the note, nor was Harvey then legally old enough to sign on his own. As he left the bank and lumbered down the street dejectedly, the manager pursued him and said he had some private funds as a manager and he would give him the loan from that. Harvey made good on the contract, paid off the loan and went on for bigger and better jobs, building roads and building up a large workforce and equipment, then moving to Picton as part of a contract to build the Glenora highway. He was so pleased with his workers there, he decided to stay. One of his accomplishments was paving every street in town for free.

Shortly after starting at the bureau, I was strolling through Shire Hall. As I passed the office of Sheriff Herb Colliver, he yelled at me to come in. He introduced himself and bluntly stated: "We haven't got anything on you yet, but I'm sure we'll get something." We went on to chat for a bit. I treated his comment as a meaningless threat, perhaps coming from a distorted County sense of humour. Herb and I went on to become good friends. When we moved out of Picton and into Cherry Valley, I pursued my dream of owning a dairy goat. Herb was particularly interested in this. He phoned me one day to ask for advice: he'd bought a complete herd of twenty or more goats. I told him he should have started small to get the hang of it, but he said it was a special auction deal and he had no choice. He put up good fences around his West Lake property and let the goats tear into clearing the land of brush and shrubs, which were abundant.

One of the most embarrassing errors I ever made was not strictly my own fault. One year, some officials decided to spark up the annual Santa Claus Parade by arranging with CFB Trenton to have the jolly old man arrive by helicopter instead of on his usual float. The Saturday of the parade, my teletype started dinging urgently with a note from my editor. He had a hold to fill on the district page and he was desperate for anything. Since Picton was the only bureau with a major event that day, he prevailed on me to write the Santa story in advance. I cautioned that there was a risk of helicopter failure or the base could get involved in some emergency situation. But I conceded and put fingers to teletype keys to paint a picture of a large crowd of parents and children at the fairgrounds, then the whirr of rotors and a speck in the sky and the helicopter landing amidst a blinding blast of snow from the rotors. I then went up to the fairgrounds to check on the situation. There was a crowd of parents and children, and plenty of snow, so the stage was set. The story was duly printed in that day's edition, but Santa was late and ultimately arrived by bus. Our story was the laughingstock of the town that day. In journalism, you cannot hide your mistakes. They are in print and always public.

About three years after I arrived, I had an offer to join the *Picton Gazette* as assistant to the late, great Phil Dodds. Bureau work was great, but I was tired of working alone all the time.

Phil and I made a good team. Originally, the plan was for Phil to retire, but once he got an assistant, retirement flew from his mind. I didn't care much. Then a dairy farmer from Cherry Valley, Harry Evans, started writing hugely humorous letters to the editor and we made him a columnist. Harry and I also became close friends, and drinking and singing buddies, alongside his agricultural mentor and neighbour, the expatriate Dane, Dan Nielsen.

The County abounded in characters in those years: Lloyd Thompson, master photographer and wartime combat photographer; Al Purdy, poet; Ann Farwell, remembered through the Milford library branch; and Dr. Sally Searles. When I went to her for a nasty cold one day, she prescribed three days in bed. I said the *Gazette* couldn't put up with that. "Do you want to work or do you want to get better?" she asked.

I remember an interview with the late Al Purdy one evening, drinking beer and watering his lakeside lawn on Roblin Lake as a result. "When a man can't piss on his own property, it's the end of the world," Purdy proclaimed.

Another character I recall was Wilkie Bailey. He drove a flatbed wagon around town peddling market produce, powered by a team of horses. When he was young, he bought a brand-new car. His first drive in it terrified him so much he parked it in a barn and left it there, sticking to horse and wagon. I'm sure someone stumbled on a real treasure in that barn at some point.

The publisher of the *Gazette* was another much-loved character around town. He had served in the Royal Flying Corps during the First World War, as a spotter—going up in a balloon-held basket to spot out enemy formations and activities. It was one of the most dangerous jobs in the war. One day, he bought himself a gasoline-powered golf cart, which he proudly drove to work, driving right up to the main entrance and parking there, dressed in his First World War long brown leather coat, helmet, and goggles. A victim of emphysema, he went into the hospital one day. I paid him a social visit and he was bouncing around his bed, putting his trousers on and off. "I'm just practising getting dressed. I hope to get out of here soon," he said. A couple of days later, he died.

Our shop foreman, Peter Cole, like most of us in the business, had a drinking problem, but he kept himself under control most of the time. If things were going wrong with any edition of the paper or part of the process, Peter would always say: "These are stirring times, Jack." I loved that line. Daisy Norton was our longest-serving staffer, basically running the front office. She could remember setting type from banks of tiny metal letters by hand in order to print something.

We took our own photographs and processed the film in a darkroom, but we relied on Mary Patterson, who had a photo studio up over a drug store on Main Street, to make prints. Often, some of our negatives were over- or under-exposed—or maybe it was our darkroom technology. Regardless, Mary could always come through with a usable print somehow. I quipped once that she could get a print off a blank negative.

And oh, the parties! Especially at election time. Harvey McFarland owned the Royal Hotel and Barney Hepburn, his reeve, managed it as his employee. For municipal elections, almost everyone in the then-ten municipalities booked large rooms for a joint party. Thus one could drink in Picton, Hillier, Wellington, Bloomfield, Hallowell, Sophiasburgh, Athol, North Marysburgh, and South Marysburgh. There was no curfew and booze flowed like a river. Thank God for a healthy liver.

I still cover events in the County as a freelancer, especially music and theatre events, and always look forward to renewing friendships from those days and making new ones.

SUMMER WAGES AT LAKESHORE LODGE

BY JANE MOON

Although I didn't fully appreciate it at the time, the summer I was sixteen I lived a true County experience as an employee of the grand lady on the lake, the historic Lakeshore Lodge. I was untrained at both waitressing and cottage cleaning, but I guess I looked young, willing to learn, and energetic in my crisp white uniform.

Most of the staff were from away and boarded in the rooms allocated for staff at the back of the main lodge. This part of the hotel did not quite live up to the elegance of the rooms in which paying guests stayed or dined. As a local girl, I had the best of both worlds: on my days off, time to go home to sleep, eat well, and watch my mom do my laundry, and when on back-to-back shifts, sleep in the shared accommodation with three other girls.

The proximity to the beach was such a bonus on our mid-afternoon breaks, when we could have a quick swim, and tan slathered in baby oil to attract the sun, not protect us from it.

As in so many of our little communities throughout the County, there were regulars who visited, or had business arrangements with, the Lodge. One such local was Jack, a single man who loved to take the girls out water-skiing when they weren't working. At the time, I thought that Jack was a kind guy giving up his time. As I recall now, through a more jaded lens, I suppose he enjoyed watching the young bikini-clad girls jumping in and out of his boat. The innocence of youth painted him more kindly.

That summer, I was too young to go to Woodstock; I was too young to keep up with my older sibling and cousins who were discovering the '60s in a whole new way. For me, it was a time of learning about life away from the shelter of my family. There was something very special about Lakeshore Lodge. I like to think that if those walls could talk, they would have shared the stories of families travelling by boat from the United States, or by train or horse and carriage, to vacation on the shores of Lake Ontario.

Sadly, a few years later, on a trip home to the County, I went back to Lakeshore Lodge to find it no longer in operation. Later, I heard there was a fire, and eventually, it was torn down. Today, when I visit and walk the grounds, I see remnants of the foundation of the main lodge and some of the cottages. The floor of the dance hall remains and prompts me to recall dancing to the jukebox with a summer love many years ago.

TREASURE AT HALLOWELL COVE

BY JANET KELLOUGH

I've never understood the wisdom of sticking a golf course on top of a cliff, especially since there always seemed to be so many bad golfers in Picton. Or maybe it's that last hole, where a misplayed ball can so easily sail over into the water. But when I was a kid, Picton Golf and Country Club provided my brother John and me with a small bonanza every summer.

Dad always had boats, and we spent as much time on them as possible. Even on a weeknight, Mum would pack up a picnic supper if the weather was nice, and as soon as Dad finished work we'd hop on the boat and go "down bay," at least a little way. Most often, we only went as far as Hallowell Cove, where we anchored out of the wind below the golf club. John and I would jump overboard as soon as the anchor hit the water, anxious to wash away the sticky sweat of a summer day. We never swam near the iron ore dock—that's where the water snakes were, and although they never bothered anyone while they were in the water, it was unpleasant to feel them slithering around our legs.

Then, while Mum was getting supper ready, we'd row the dinghy over to the shore just beneath the golf club. There was treasure there: golf balls. Some of them were easy pickings, lying in shallow water close to shore.

Others were further out and we had to dive down deep to even see them, but we could retrieve them if we held our breath long enough.

The quality varied considerably. Some of them were pretty roughed up, or had been in the water for a long time. But recent additions to the bottom were in good shape, and there always seemed to be a few really bad golfers who bought really good balls.

"Those are mine," my brother would say of the good ones, even if it was me who'd found them.

"No they aren't," I'd say, and we'd squabble over them all through supper and on into the evening, even as the sun was setting and we pulled anchor to head for home.

I don't know why I argued over it—it was always John who sought out the golfers he knew and offered to sell them the second-hand balls. The ones in the poorest condition were worth only a nickel or two, but the good ones could fetch as much as seventy-five cents, especially if he could find one of the bad golfers who'd lost a ball like it in the first place.

He usually gave me at least some of the proceeds—because he knew I'd complain to Mum if he didn't—but I knew it was never a fifty-fifty split. It was my first introduction to the concept of the middleman. I didn't really care. For me, the money wasn't nearly as important as the fun of diving for golf balls.

THE SWEETEST TRADITION

BY KAREN PALMER

The chatter started even before my first day on the job. As the newest member of the County's community development team, I was warned I'd have to wear the maple mascot suit at that year's Maple in the County.

Hazing, I think they call it.

The festival is considered the County's sweetest tradition. It's typically the last weekend in March, a chance to visit any of a dozen or more maple-producing farms, and has grown exponentially in popularity, pulling in thousands of families from Toronto, Ottawa, and beyond.

My eyes must have widened in horror.

I can't be the only one who spies some poor sap in a mascot costume and thinks: *That poor sap. What went wrong in their life to lead them to this?*

A gangly teen in a cross-eyed foot-long hot dog absolutely melting at a little league ball game; a mute mobile phone being led around by a corporate stooge. An utterly unidentifiable person swaddled in plushy fabrics made to resemble a unicorn, an onion, a pizza slice. All of them getting kidney-punched by third-grade hooligans. Move in too close and you can see their desperation through the mesh peephole, their eyes practically screaming: "Don't look at me! Do not look at me!"

I had just moved to the County—by the time of Maple in the County, I would have been there only three months. I knew almost no one. I pictured a shiny red unitard. I pictured hipsters in buffalo check pushing in for an ironic selfie. Kids dripping with maple syrup bursting into tears at the sight of me.

I mean, I was in my early forties. That's the kind of public humiliation that in your twenties is considered "character building." In your forties, it's just pathetic.

So when I was told—repeatedly—that I'd be suiting up for the media event, I rebuffed the idea as politely and as firmly as possible.

No way.

Mabel, as it turned out, was a jaunty red maple leaf, each of her bright eyes ringed by three coquettish eyelashes, with a darling little button nose and a wide, welcoming smile. She was made of the same material used to make hockey bags, with a square of matching mesh fabric to act as a lookout. To keep the points of her leaf crisp, she'd been framed with cut-down hockey sticks.

She went over the head, with assistance, and the bottom of the leaf reached to mid-thigh. She weighed as much as a sturdy toddler.

And apparently "everyone" had worn her.

As the date drew closer, I surreptitiously looked through the image files. There were my colleague Rebecca's long dancer legs in skinny jeans and tall boots from the previous year's news conference. There was my colleague Ashley, gamely posing in the suit, having been helped to the ground during a photo shoot at the park next to Shire Hall.

And still I thought: No way.

Today's Mabel is actually a reincarnation.

Maple in the County was started before *Toronto Life* magazine discovered the area. Before some of Toronto's top tattooed chefs migrated toward the bucolic County shores for farm-to-table cuisine. Before The June's clarion call to "rosé all day." As difficult as it is to believe, there was a time when the County had to convince visitors to veer off the highway and visit our island paradise. That job fell to the team at Taste the County.

Mabel was their brainchild, and Maple in the County a festival they avidly promoted as the beginning of the tourist season. And it made perfect sense. In 1849, maple tappers in Hillier alone produced 34,000 pounds of sugar. A decade later, maple producers across the County produced a whopping 219,000 pounds of sugar. That's nearly 110,000 litres of syrup.

Why not showcase the County's long history in the maple syrup business?

At some point, a maple head was born, hewn out of foam by Buddha Dog's Andrew Hunter. She was dubbed Mabel, a somewhat dowdy yet perfectly serviceable name. Like Teddy Ruxpin and the Koosh ball, she existed in a time before the Internet. I could find no photos of her, but apparently she made the rounds, enticing local people to put on their woolies and venture out to a sugarbush on the last weekend of March.

She had a few flaws, according to Grace Nyman, now my colleague at the County, but back then a member of the Taste team. Since Mabel was made of foam, she was absorbent. And since her time to shine was in early spring, she was like a giant Q-tip, eagerly sopping up any flower-bringing showers.

In a pinch, Grace asked her mother, Patricia Smit, if she could devise and sew an upgrade. Grace's sister, Virginia deVries, happened to be living with their parents at the time. She seized the challenge, sourcing yards and yards of fire-engine red, waterproof fabric. They sketched out a pattern. Grace's father, Klass Smit, engineered the frame.

"It was so creative," Grace told me. "They really went beyond the call of duty."

When Mabel made her debut, she was an instant hit. At a press conference, the Q-tip disappeared, ostensibly for some minor elective surgery, and reappeared a beautiful swan.

The new Mable was a bit heavy, but wherever she went, people flocked to have a photo with her. Rebecca Mackenzie, also formerly of Taste, guided a willing volunteer dressed as Mabel into local restaurants, earning calls and cheers. Tabitha Kay wore her for three seasons. Grace's son Carter took a turn in the suit. Sean McKinney's daughter answered the call for volunteers. Trevor Crowe's daughter Mercedes was volun-told to wear the costume, moving from site to site during the festival.

Wherever she went, Mabel was a magnet, Grace says. "Mabel is in many, many family photos taken during Maple in the County." They stitched up some cloth bags and Mabel became a local version of the Easter Bunny, distributing maple candies wherever she went. Even young men were up for a photo with the vivid red character.

It's those eyelashes, I tell you.

I heard more and more about Mabel as Maple in the County drew closer.

Early in the year, maple producers—not farmers, producers—gather to discuss their offerings, make plans for signage, maps, and marketing, and to agree on a date for a media event.

We met at Rob and Sally Peck's kitchen table: myself, Ron and Janice Hubbs, Clifford Foster, Nora Westervelt, Joshua Feddema, Justin VanNiejenhui, Todd and Michelle Vader, Jessie and Chris Armstrong, John and Michelle Nyman, Phil and Brittany Roblin, Justin Williams. There in spirit were John and Sacha Squair and Jane Breakell and Brian Walt. The Vader family has been producing syrup since 1910. Clifford's Fosterholm Farms has been boiling sap since 1924, with lines snaking through more than seven thousand trees at the entrance to Sandbanks Provincial Park.

During Maple in the County, a dozen maple producers open their farms to the public, inviting them in to watch them tap and boil sap, selling not just syrup but butter tarts, maple-glazed pulled pork, waffles, pancakes, maple butter, taffy, maple sugar, and the diabetes-inducing Walt Drop. Named for Walt's Sugar Shack, they're a battered and deep-fried maple cookie and yes, they are glorious.

Of all the festivals and events held in the County—and there are *many*—it is the most authentically "County," with half-ton trucks parked on the roadside and Carhartt overalls worn for practicality, not fashion. Tractor buckets are filled with canned goods for the local food bank. Volunteer firefighters flip pancakes. Plates of sausage links and enamel jugs of syrup are doled out by men with gnarled knuckles, fundraisers for service clubs that help keep this community going. It's the embodiment of what draws so many people here.

"You ready?" Ron Hubbs asked me, a teasing twinkle in his eye. (In fairness, in my experience, Ron always has a teasing twinkle in his eye.)

My actual responsibility—the thing I was paid to do—was organize the media event. Since Taste closed, the maple producers have organized the event themselves with a smidge of support from the County: we dream up creative ways to gather all the producers together for a cutesy photo op. One year, it was letters spelling out Maple in the County on sap buckets. Another year, it was toasting wine glasses of syrup. For the festival's sweet sixteen, it was a stack of pancakes with candles on top.

The winter I was involved, Korea was hosting the Olympic games. Canada was rolling out a new grading system for syrup, with designations for golden, amber, and dark amber. It was decided that we'd mimic the Olympic medals and showcase the new colour coding.

That's how I found myself up at eleven the night before the media event sewing red ribbons through discs of yellow, orange, and brown foamboard. I discovered midway through that I'd been too miserly in my ribbon cutting and had made a dozen "medals" whose straps wouldn't fit over my head.

It was somewhere in the unpicking of the stitches that I began to think I might as well do it. I might as well wear the costume.

I didn't want to be a diva. And if the producers were game enough to pose in front of people they knew with these cheesy medals around their necks, I could stand anonymously among them in a beloved costume and help make a decent photo to announce the event.

So, after Ron's warm welcome and the mayor's speech and Justin's inspiring words about the future of farming, Rebecca and I disappeared behind the Roblin's shiny reverse osmosis machine and settled Mabel on my shoulders. Rebecca put her own red Canada mitts on my hands and led me into the photo. I managed to nearly knock over two people on my way through, still adjusting to the width of my shoulder pads.

We stood for a few snaps. I noticed Mabel smelled like a well-worn, under-laundered sweat sock. She'd been stored in the old jail cells at Shire Hall, and her hockey sticks weren't as sturdy as they used to be. In the photos, the bulge of my head straining against the fabric is clear—she wasn't resting on my shoulders so much as my forehead.

Then Rebecca, ever social-media minded, led me outside. Just one more photo, for the County's Instagram page.

I was stupidly wearing rain boots, despite two inches of snow, and jeans with their hem rolled high. The thin socks inside the black boots did absolutely nothing to protect against the damp cold, but I thought they'd look particularly fetching against the red of Mabel's suit.

I was freshly returned from the Philippines, where I'd lived for a few years and had gotten into the trend of jump shots. You try to get airborne just as the shutter closes. It's ridiculous, but it does make it look like you're having the time of your life.

So I did that.

My toes were basically ice cubes, but they launched me skyward all the same. For extra effect, I waved the little mitts like jazz hands. In truth, I couldn't really see what I was doing. Every time I jumped, the costume shifted, covering my eyes. And when I landed, it came down heavily on my head, causing me to bow a little. All I knew was that Rebecca, laughing, kept giving me stage directions: More to the left! A little higher! One more time!

When I finally looked out, a little breathless, there was a row of photographers. In the photos, it really does look like Mabel is jumping for joy.

That's Mabel's appeal, Grace says.

"It's her smile and her eyes. And the red. It looks really sharp if you wear black underneath it."

Take note, whoever comes next. It's the sweetest tradition. And you've gotta do it.

FIRE AND FROST

BY KIMBALL LACEY

You can see the frost coming in. It always travels from the east side of the vineyard to the west. You know you're going to lose the crop if you don't do anything, so you're out there doing something to make yourself feel better. But you're never one hundred percent sure that it's going to work.

May 11, 2010 was one of those nights. I started preparing the day before, getting hay bales out all over the field. I put out close to two hundred bales for that night. At about twelve-thirty in the morning I got the alarm saying the temperature had gone down to two degrees in the vineyard. I got up, made coffee, went out to the field and started lighting up the hay bales with a big roofing torch. It's not just the smoke you're after: you get some residual heat from the burning hay bales as well. We've got a little pattern that we set up where we light up the headlands first, and then, as the night progresses, we start lighting more and more bales around the perimeter of the field. You get this amazing cloud of smoke overhead from the burning hay. It kind of looks like a little war zone out there.

There's no break during the night. You're up from the time your alarm goes off until eight or nine in the morning, still burning, and if there's a risk of frost after that you've got to go around and reload the whole field. That night we went through about three hundred bales of hay, just constantly feeding fires, walking around the field. You probably walk a good five or six miles throughout the night because you never stop.

My dad sat down at one end in the lowest spot. We kept a bonfire going there, so he manned that for us during the night. Two to three people and that's it, covering as much ground as possible. The last couple that I've done, it's just been me out in the ten-acre field, walking the perimeter with a pitchfork.

That night, it worked. We saved the whole crop, didn't lose anything. It was a good night.

On the other hand, May 22–23, 2015 was a brutal one. We started burning at eleven-thirty. I remember the exact time. The notification appeared on my phone, and I got out in the field and started lighting the fires right away. We fed the fires all night. I had to make three hay runs, going to another field where we store the hay to get more. We went through eight hundred bales that night. By three-thirty in the morning it was already minus one, and by five-thirty the temperature in the vineyard was down to minus six.

Nothing was going to save the crop that night. Even people who had fans blowing warm air around their vineyards still lost fifty to sixty percent of their crops, because the colder it gets, the smaller the area the fans can cover. We burned, and we still lost sixty percent of everything. It was a brutal night.

A GRAND MYSTERY

BY LAURIE SCOTT

Antiques allow us to glimpse the past, to connect in some way with those who came before us. But is there more to it? Can objects themselves hold spiritual imprints of their former owners? Is there some kind of psychic energy that lingers in relics once fiercely possessed? These are questions I found myself asking in 1969.

The square grand piano my mother bought at an auction fifty years ago was a beast. Six feet long and rectangular in shape, it weighed in at around a thousand pounds. For months, my parents worked on restoring it to its former glory, patiently stripping away the thick layers of black paint that covered the original finish. Gradually, the beauty emerged, and along with it, a mystery that would soon cause quite a stir.

When the project was completed, the piano was moved from the garage into our house at 17 Main West where, surrounded on three sides by tall bay windows, it struck a stately pose in the front parlour. Some surprises had been discovered beneath the old paint. First, there was the gorgeous rosewood. Then, the lettering above the keyboard. I don't recall the company name that was displayed there, but under that name was a year—1838. The provenance of the piano was unknown, and I tried to imagine its long history—where it had been and whose hands might have played it over the previous 130 years.

The ivories were still in good shape, but a piano of that age and era is difficult to keep in tune, so it became more a part of the decor than a functional instrument. There were two other pianos in the house at the time, so my mother, a talented pianist, was only mildly disappointed that her latest acquisition was not pitch-perfect. The old square grand, polished and gleaming once again, occupied its prime spot fronting the bay windows in silence. Until it didn't.

I was a teenager at the time, and on weekends, frequently a night owl. On this particular night, I was in my bedroom, reading. It was late, just past midnight, and the other residents of the house—my parents, my brother and my grandmother—were asleep, having gone to bed at around nine o'clock. My room was situated near the top of the main staircase that led down to the front hall. French doors opened from there to the front parlour. I was closing my book when the silence broke: the sound that came up those stairs was deliberate, clear, and loud.

I heard two notes—a high note followed two seconds later by a lower one. The notes were the same, but the pitches were three or four octaves apart. If I had to guess, I would identify the notes as C6, followed by C2 (C4 being middle C). Both were held, as though a finger had remained pressed on each key while the sustain pedal was engaged. This sudden utterance from the old piano so frightened me that I immediately ran to my bedroom door and flicked the lever above the handle into the locked position. I stood there, breath-less, wondering what was happening and what I should do about it. I knew that it wasn't my brother messing with my head. As a paraplegic, getting himself out of bed and down the noisy elevator without being heard was not only impossible, but absurd.

My mind raced with possibilities, but I could come up with only one sensible idea: someone had broken into the house and was sending us a message. This was no ordinary intruder. This one wanted to announce his presence, to taunt us, before coming upstairs to murder us all. But who would do such a thing? If memory serves correctly, this happened in the months follow-ing the Manson family murder spree in California, and although Picton was a far cry from LA, that would've been more than enough to fuel my imagination with thoughts of our impending deaths.

I wanted desperately to run to my parents' room next door and wake them. Just maybe there was a chance we could escape or fight off whoever it was. Helter skelter, this was bad! I couldn't bring myself to open the door. The piano had fallen silent, and although I'd heard no movement on the creaky stairs, I envisioned the intruder grinning evilly in the dark hallway outside my door, waiting for me to emerge.

I sat on my bed, listening intently for any sound—musical notes, footfalls, murderous screams. Finally, when hours had passed and I'd heard nothing of the sort, I convinced myself that whoever had been at the keyboard downstairs had left. It didn't occur to me at the time that the piano might be haunted, and that our uninvited guest might be a ghost.

The following morning, greatly relieved that we were all still alive, I told everyone what had occurred during the night. Ideas were suggested. From my grandmother: perhaps it was the cat traipsing across the keyboard. No. I described again the sustained nature of the notes and how they were the same, octaves apart. Our cat was not that clever. My father: perhaps heat from the registers on the floor nearby had caused old strings to expand or snap and release the hammers. No. This was not the kind of sound I heard. The keys were played. My mother: perhaps I'd been dreaming. No. I'd been sitting up, about to turn off the light.

With no reasonable explanation forthcoming, the incident was relegated to the realm of unsolved mysteries, and over the next short while more or less forgotten. We did, however, find ourselves casting nervous glances at the piano when the room seemed too quiet, and at times, my mother felt an uncomfortable presence when she was alone with it.

A couple of weeks after my unsettling experience, it was my brother's turn. Something roused him from his sleep in the wee hours of the morning and, wide awake, he heard three piano chords play in succession—deliberate, clear and sustained. Not having the option to jump out of bed and lock his door, he lay there, scared and anxious, listening as I had for something else to happen. I suppose his only comfort was in knowing that this ghost hadn't seemed interested in harming anyone on its previous visit. The rest of us slept through the episode, unaware that our mysterious intruder had returned.

Never before had any of us felt the presence of ghostly entities in our home. The house was old, the original part having been built in 1814 and completely enclosed by additions one hundred years later, but until the antique piano took residence, nothing strange had ever spooked us. If there were any further middle-of-the-night visits from our phantom pianist, no one was awake to hear them.

I'm not sure how long the piano was in our home before my mother decided to get rid of it. A year or two, perhaps. It was in the home of my oldest brother for a short time before being sold to a former owner of the *Picton Gazette*. Its fate after that is unknown. It would be interesting to track down the buyers and find out if anything similar has happened to them, but how does one ask that question? Hey, you know that piano my family sold you? Have you ever heard it play all by itself in the middle of the night? Oh, didn't we mention that? Yes, it's a little haunted.

Perhaps our piano wanted to be played, not just displayed. Maybe the spirit of some previous owner, delighted with its renewal, came back to admire it and reminisce. Or perhaps that mysterious energy resided in the house, not the piano. It's possible that my brother and I were uniquely receptive to psychic energy. If there is a more mundane explanation, it continues to elude me. I've mentally filed it, along with a few other experiences, under UXP—unexplained phenomena.

Regardless of its strange behaviour, the old rosewood piano was a thing of beauty. One hundred eighty-one years ago, someone somewhere tuned it for the first time, so that someone else could sit down to play their prized new possession. I wonder if it still feels the touch of human hands. I hope so.

ROUGHING IT IN GREENBUSH

BY LORIS WAGER as told to Krista Dalby

I was born in 1948. I grew up here, on Clarke Road. It wasn't Clarke Road then, it was just the road. These secondary roads didn't have names, they were only named probably in the '70s or later on. I've lived here all my life, slept in the same bedroom, never any other place.

Our one-room school was considered one of the worst schools in the County: S.S. No. 2, Hallowell, Upper Greenbush. A lot of teachers didn't want to teach there. I think we were kind of little devils, really. The kids weren't bad. There was only one kid who was really bad, he used to keep a paring knife in his desk and all the kids were scared of him. The police would be out there every couple of months to get him for something—he stabbed kids in town, he got in a lot of trouble. He later went to prison, but his buddy, he became a preacher. The ironic thing was that bad kid became a preacher too, later in life.

I spent twenty-one years in school. I failed Grade One and Grade Three and Grade Four and Grade Ten. I wasn't a smart kid. I liked history, I liked geography, that was it. I only passed spelling once in my life. It didn't matter how much we studied, I just couldn't grasp spelling. My only good subject was daydreaming! I've still got all my report cards, right till Grade Twelve. Even though I failed, I've still got 'em all. You look at 'em, they say, "He didn't pay much attention. He'll never amount to anything." Ha!

But I liked that school far better than high school, because you knew everybody, you knew all the families. It was the '70s when they quit that one-room school. I was the last generation that went there for eight grades.

School was fun because we played a lot of games. There was a hollow that was dug out in the ground and we used to have a door, so the bigger kids used to take us smaller kids and throw us in the hollow and put the door on top of us and jump up and down on the door. They didn't let you out unless you were crying. I was never old enough that I got on top of the door—I was always the one underneath it.

There were around twenty-eight kids. One year, we had six different teachers. The first teacher, she got pregnant at Christmastime, then we had a supply teacher, then we had another supply teacher, then we had another teacher, and the next teacher had a nervous breakdown and she had to quit. We were just a bad school. I think the reason they considered us bad was because I think those days teachers chose the schools they liked, and we were the kind they didn't want. I think probably because we weren't the richest part.

From the school we'd walk across the fields to the army camp. The army people lived in those barracks there and they used to have a canteen, so when we'd have twenty-five cents we'd walk over and get a pop. We just got carried away one day and we never got back till three o'clock, and we really got heck from the teacher! The army used to have manoeuvres over there by the school and they used to put this black wire through the woods for their communications, 'cause they didn't have walkie-talkies, so they used those wires to go from one walkie-talkie to another. So we used to go over as kids and take stones and cut the wires in two. But funny thing, they never gave us heck for it. They had to go out and figure out where to repair the wire, fix it back up, and go on with their business.

The army, once and a while they'd bring over baseball bats and stuff like that to the school. They brought us over boxing gloves one time, but they didn't last for long because the teacher took them away from us 'cause one girl threw one of the boxing gloves down the toilet. We did have a lot of fun at school.

They got us new desks—have you ever seen *Anne of Green Gables*? We used to have those desks. And then they bought brand-new desks, but they only got six or seven. So my older brother, he got one, and he carved his initials in the top of the desk by the inkwell. So then after he got out of school, my other brother got that desk and he carved his initials underneath, and after that, I got the desk and I carved my initials underneath. The last year I was there they sent the desks away and got them all redone. They sanded our names off. I always wished I'd stolen the desk ... and the bell ... and the strap.

In those days, if you were left-handed, the teacher would give you the strap. You couldn't be left-handed or write left-handed; if you wrote left-handed you blotted all your ink. You had to write upside-down.

One time we was playing Killy-Callie-Over and one of the balls hit the teacher's car and broke one of the markers off, and nobody knew who did it, or nobody would tell who did it, so the teacher strapped us all. That's called The Way It Was.

Every year, we went for Christmas trees. The big boys, we'd go up to where the Old Milford Road comes out to get a Christmas tree for the school. You had to be in Grade Seven or Grade Eight, because you had to use an axe or a saw. We'd have a Christmas concert in the school, it was a lot of fun, we'd put on plays and all that stuff. We didn't have angels in those days. I remember one time Dad dressed up as Santa Claus and he came down with the horses and a sleigh and gave out Christmas presents.

Everybody looked forward to Valentine's Day 'cause you'd always give the girls you liked the best valentines. There were two girls, I couldn't make up my mind which one I liked the best—needless to say, I didn't end up with either one! At Halloween we'd walk all over. I dressed like a clown, like the one I probably was. We just dressed up as anything, I guess, we didn't buy costumes, we just made them. We didn't have flashlights, but we had good eyes back then. Once and a while you'd fall down, but I never done any damage.

I can remember when as kids we used to take a stick and put two little wheels on it, like tricycle wheels, and we'd push them around, pretend like they were tractors.

Dad'd be plowing with the tractor and we'd be going up and down pushing this stick. We didn't have a lot of toys in those days. You kept your toys your whole life.

I remember Mom cooking Christmas dinner on the wood stove, the wind was coming up underneath the house and the air was lifting the linoleum up—it was like walking on a cloud! One year when we were small, I remember Dad only had seven dollars to buy Christmas presents, so he bought us this aluminum flying saucer that you ride on down the hill ... I've still got it. It's in the woodhouse beside the door. You remember the Christmas presents at times when you had little. That's what you remember through your whole life.

WOOL ROAD

BY LOUISE BAZETT-JONES

There's an unadvertised event that takes place here several times a year. It isn't written up in tourist magazines—never will be. But if you're lucky, maybe you've seen it. Maybe you've even had the good fortune to take part. A festival? No. A gourmet dinner? No. A parade, you ask? Well, almost. Let me tell you about the herding of the sheep, yes, thousands of them, along these County roads. It's a forced migration of the gentlest sort.

My experience with this great migration started one winter's day four years ago. I was new to the County then. I believe I'd never seen more than three sheep together—and that was at the old Riverdale Zoo in downtown Toronto. But I'd definitely left city life, was happily installed here, and ready for a feast of country experiences. As it happened, I decided to walk east along County Road 7, enjoying the quiet of a Sunday winter morning. I was padding happily down the middle of the road; heavy snowfalls and the local ploughs had conspired to make the embankments over three feet tall. And then it became apparent that the morning's quiet was being eroded by a distinctive, low rumble, interrupted by shouting and dogs barking. It was then that I looked up and saw a wall of sheep barrelling down the road right at me. Sheep literally filled the road from one bank to the other, and they were coming fast. What to do?

Just in time, I jumped over the snow bank and watched in awe and delight as a thousand, no, thousands of sheep trotted past. Halfway through the parade, a bearded man on a quad bike slowed down as he passed. "Yup, they're my sheep—taking them to a new field further west. Sorry to have startled you," he said. And then as he revved the quad, still within earshot, he quipped, "Just a typical Sunday morning in the County!"

Yes, it was, except that the usually bare pavement, though never as pristine as Yonge and Bloor, was definitely un-pristine.

And that was fine by me.

That was the beginning of my relationship with Matt the shepherd. Later that year, he must have noticed that we don't own a riding lawn mower. In fact, we don't own a lawn mower at all. The wild grasses in fields around our house dance in the wind. I guess it caught his attention, so one day he knocked on the door and asked if he could bring his sheep to our place. Since then, we've had the pleasure of sheep visiting the property at regular intervals throughout the year. The formula's simple: they eat the grass and leave behind free fertilizer. It's what we call a win-win situation.

More recently, I've been invited to help with the migration. Matt's sheep make regular trips along County roads to obtain fresh pasture and, by spring, arrive on Waupoos Island for lambing. You should know that a successful herding event takes a lot of people; to stand along roads, guard driveways, block possible escape routes, and diplomatically direct traffic. You may have heard that sheep like to meander. In fact, I'd say they're experts at the art of the lightning-quick disappearing act. And they do this in groups. So your job as a herding volunteer is to keep—that is, try to keep—those sheep on the road and out of people's yards and fields. Especially challenging are the beautifully manicured front lawns; sheep migrate to such venues like children to chocolate. Turns out, they love green, and my theory is that they know where all the master gardeners live.

My latest herding technique is to stand at the edge of a road looking like an animated scarecrow, arms out, flapping the air wildly. On a recent migration, as I was manning an intersection where one road led to Milford, a bystander whimsically suggested that I was Milford's last hope. I didn't have to worry, though; the sheep kept to their designated route.

Picture this: you're at the bottom of a hill. At the top of the hill, you see a phalanx of sheep. Row upon row of them, they fill the road. And now those in the front line are staring right at you. Yes, little, inexperienced you, in the bright orange vest, standing at the bottom of the hill. And then, God help you, the sheep begin to accelerate down the hill toward you. Trotting and baaing: here they come. It's just you and the sheep now. Luckily, they flow right past like a woolen river. It's at this moment you realize—with great relief, I might add—that you haven't been trampled, the sheep have stayed on the road, you're alive and standing, and what's more, you're enjoying the parade. Usually, it's a group endeavour. There are many experienced men and women on the team, some on quads—and at least two border collies.

But there was one time—I might say a more challenging time—when I was assigned the task of protecting a gorgeous white farmhouse surrounded by one of those superbly green master gardens. In my memory, the lawn was a sea of emerald with an abundance of flowers nestled in carefully manicured beds. Hundreds of sheep had already flowed past and I was happily complacent. Then, just as I thought everything was under control, a dozen sheep saw an opportunity not to be missed, ran off the road, and headed straight for the lawn and the flower beds. I ran after them, of course, waving madly. I hooted and hollered. I begged. The sheep took no notice and I watched, helpless, as they began to tuck in to a master garden all-you-can-eat-buffet.

And this, my friend, is when the miracle happened. Somewhere in the window of time between my last desperate thought and my next breath, the two border collies, twin Supermen, jumped into action. Like canine billiard cues, they nosed and poked the sheep, running low to the ground, this way and that. And in less than thirty seconds, the dogs placed all of the sheep—and I mean all of them—back onto the road. The next thing I knew, all two thousand sheep were standing peacefully in a nearby field, just where they were supposed to be.

Soon the dogs were resting, content in a warm truck, their job done. And I rested too, along with the dogs and the twenty neighbours—farmers, friends, and photographers—everyone who'd helped with the great migration, enjoying homemade sandwiches and hot tea together at the side of the road. And I realized that this herding event is really an ordinary event that makes the County a community—and this just a typical Sunday morning in the County.

COMING FROM AWAY

BY LYNNE DONOVAN

It's interesting to me how the County has always been a destination for people who are from away; it's not simply a trend that started ten or so years ago. When I look at the makeup of the congregation of St. Andrew's, for example, some of our oldest members arrived from the British Isles in the '20s, the '40s even as late as the '50s. People haven't just been coming here in the last twenty years, but were showing up sixty, seventy, ninety years ago.

One of our oldest members, Anne Raby, is about to turn ninety-eight. Her family was brought here in 1928, when she was seven years old, as immigrants, almost refugees from Ireland. She, her four siblings, and her parents, Thomas and Margaret Wilkinson, were sponsored by the church because Ireland was not an easy place to make a living at that time. They arrived on a boat, and were picked up at the train station in Picton—there was a train from Belleville three times a week—by Reverend Scott, the minister of St. Andrew's Presbyterian Church. I believe her father found work in a hardware store. Her mother, her sisters, and her brother were all employed by the Young family who owned the house that is now the Claremont. Then, when the depression hit, they were let go.

Anne Raby, who went on to become a Bell employee, and was in fact a manager of one of the Bell offices up in

Belleville, could tell you a lot, given the amount of time she spent managing party lines around the County.

Others came as war brides, sixty to seventy years ago, and have such remarkable histories, having created new lives for themselves here. I can remember a woman associated with the congregation who grew up in Glasgow. She met her husband, Oran Greatrix, who was from the County, because they were both lined up to buy fish and chips. Of course, it was wartime, and Scotland and Britain were crawling with soldiers from different parts of the Empire. When he asked her out, she agreed to go out with him, and then, at one point, probably thinking that she might not see him again, she agreed to marry him. Then he disappeared. He was sent to Italy, where he lost an eye—then lo and behold showed up on her doorstep again. So he came home, and nine months later, she was shipped over on a boat with all kinds of other war brides. She showed up at the train station in Belleville, in the middle of the night, in January. It was absolutely freezing and she wasn't quite sure if the man that she'd agreed to marry was going to pick her up or not. But they were married here in the County and went on to have forty years together before he died. She was always homesick for Scotland, but this was her community based on the choices that she'd made.

People come with different experiences and different core values. It's part of what makes living in the County so interesting.

AN AL PURDY TRIPTYCH

BY MARION CASSON

Al and the Book Sales

When I first started as curator of the Ameliasburgh Township Museum, I got a call from Al. He would bring me over a box of books for sale in the museum gift shop, all autographed, and he would like cash for them. I had seen Al at Art on the Fence, where he strolled around with the organizer, Barbara Whelan, his shirt open to his navel, so I wasn't really surprised when he arrived at ten in the morning smelling slightly of scotch. The books came almost yearly and I wish I had kept some of them.

Al and the Post Office

The post office for the hamlet was located in Mrs. Sills' sunporch on the Main Street of Ameliasburgh. Mrs. Sills, who took over the postmistress job from her mother-in-law, had some little dogs that she dearly loved. They were given free rein to be wherever they liked and to do whatever they had to. One hot summer day, when it was clear that the puppies had been in the sunporch, Al and I arrived at about the same time. Mrs. Sills was at the counter, deep in conversation with one of the local ladies. She stopped long enough to acknowledge us ... Oh, Mrs. Casson there is a package for the museum, and a letter from your publisher, Mr. Purdy. She had us—we were trapped. After that, I tried to pick up the mail on shady days.

The Last Time I Saw Al

One morning at the museum, I got a call from Al. As usual, he would be bringing over some books. We talked for a while, and I complimented him on the fact that the community had named the road leading down to the Harry Smith Conservation Area, where there is a pioneer cemetery, in his honour. He quoted Blake in response: "The patches of glory lead but to the grave." He is buried in that cemetery.

THE MEAT ROLL

BY MAX SOULIERE

"Your hat," I hissed. "Your hat!"

In the nick of time, I caught Kyle's attention and he pulled off his hat. Traditionally, wearing your hat in a Legion hall is punishable by buying a round for the house, and with the Royal Canadian Legion's Picton Branch rapidly filling up it would've been an expensive round. The reason for the big crowd: the Meat Roll!

In the three years since Donna and I moved to the County, we've participated in every tradition and local activity offered. Festival of Trees, seed swap, scavenger hunt … we'd done them all. We'd even done a Horn Trip or two! And since Kyle and Cherie had bought the place around the corner a year later, they'd joined us in all the fun. So it was on a grey November day, just an hour after having watched the Santa Claus parade, that we adjourned to Branch 78 to participate in another County event. In retrospect, Kyle should've donned his cap, paid for a round and walked out, for he was about to run afoul of a County tradition as mysterious as the Marysburg Vortex!

From the beginning, I was vaguely uneasy. After all, the term "Meat Roll" is a little creepy. It evokes either something kinky or downright unsanitary—or both. I've been to a local buck and doe party and seen a game of musical chairs nearly turn into a donnybrook, so I knew anything was possible. We were about to find out.

The central piece of Meat Roll technology turned out to be a big roulette wheel numbered from one to ninety-six. Players paid two dollars per spin, each spin was recorded on a chalk board, and the highest spins won meat—in this case a turkey, a ham, and a flank steak. Easy as pie. Since Cherie had gone home to tend to her dogs, it was left to Kyle, Donna, and me to carry the torch for our group. We decided to get our spins in early so we could enjoy some Legion-priced beverages and really soak up the flavour of this County tradition. We bought five spins each and took our places at the head of the long line of hopefuls. The place was hopping as the game began.

Donna led off. Incredibly, she spun up a ninety! She was in with a shout! I went next and to my delight landed a ninety-two! I began to salivate at the thought of free meat. Not to be outdone, Kyle threw down a ninety-four! That score just had to be a winner. We fist-pumped our way back to our seats, trying to control our excitement. There were many spins to come, but we were in this thing. Many, many, many spins later, a woman matched Kyle's top score. I was bumped back to third, and Donna was knocked off the podium. Still, we were in the meat. It was at about this time that Cherie returned, and so was witness to what followed.

All that remained was the spin-off for first between Kyle and his adversary. I was asked to join them at the meat table. Kyle spun first. Forty-eight. Not good enough. His competitor landed a sixty-eight. Always the gentleman, Kyle congratulated her on the win.

After all, second place was pretty good, and at least he'd beaten me.

She stepped to the table to claim her prize. As the winner, she had her choice. "I'll take the turkey," she said, and the guy from Goodfellow dutifully bagged her bird. It was a wonderful prize to win, with Christmas just a month away.

Up stepped Kyle. "I guess I'll take the ham," he said.

"No you won't," said the guy behind the meat table.

"What?"

"No, you won't. You lost. This guy picks next," he said, and pointed at me.

I felt badly for Kyle but I was not about to look a gift ham in the mouth. I pounced. "I'll take the ham" I said, and the guy handed me my prize.

Before Kyle could speak, the emcee took over.

"And now for the mystery spin," he said. Kyle was dumbfounded. Mystery spin? What's this? Before he could ask for an explanation, the wheel was spun, a number came up and the chalkboard was consulted. The lucky attendee who'd come closest to that number claimed third place. The emcee announced a twenty-minute break, the chalkboard was erased, and the round was over.

We returned to our table, me with my prize, and Kyle with nothing but questions. Like "What the...?" and "How the...?" The crux of his confusion was this: he'd tied for first and lost to only one person. So why no ham for Kyle? Why no flank steak? We had no answers, so while I basked in the glory of my locally grown, never-frozen, bone-in, eight-pound ham, Kyle went looking for an answer. The one he brought back was this:

At 11:53 p.m. on Monday July 4, 2016, a fire was reported at the old location of the Legion. Thanks to quick work by PEC firefighters, damage was confined to one room, but some artifacts and furnishings were lost. Among those items was the original roulette wheel used for the Meat Roll.

Now, the Meat Roll was always a big deal, but that original wheel was not. In fact, the numbers on the old wheel only went up to fourteen! As a result, tie scores were the norm, and nine-way and ten-way ties for first, second, and third were common. All those tied for first would spin off and, barring more ties, one of them would win some meat. The rest went begging. Same for second and third. When they replaced the wheel destroyed in the fire, tie scores were much less common, but the rule remained the same; there was no reason to change it. County logic was at work here and Kyle was out of luck.

As you can imagine, this explanation did not sit well with him. He easily made hamburger of the logic, which he felt had robbed him of his meat. He'd spun a ninety-four, for cryin' out loud!

After a few minutes listening to Kyle's complaints, the rest of us ran out of sympathy, and so his day got a little worse. I announced that I'd decided to give my ham a name. And that name was Kyle! Donna, Cherie and I embraced this christening with gusto, and the ham, pork, and hog jokes rained down. Kyle proved that day, and for the next week or so, that he was a very good sport.

We could now cross the Meat Roll off our bucket list. Donna and I lovingly carried Kyle the Ham to his new residence in my freezer. A few weeks later, the four of us gathered around our table. And of course, we ate Kyle for dinner. We had a delicious, laugh-filled meal and afterward we all agreed that Kyle was a real ham.

~~GWM LOOKING FOR LOVE IN PEC~~
~~GWM LOOKING TO GET LUCKY IN PEC~~
GWM LOOKING FOR SOMEONE TO TALK TO IN PEC

BY MICHAEL SOLBERG SCHELLENBERG

I moved to Prince Edward County the first day of January 2018. I had become enchanted with the place fifteen years earlier when I spent a couple summers visiting friends with digs in Cherry Valley. Little Bluff and Long Dog wine haunt my dreams ... I always thought it would make a darn fine place to hang my hat.

A refugee from an almost twenty-year marriage in Toronto, I was keen to get away from the daily reminders of the life I had led. Being a creature of impulsive, exuberant action, on one particularly construction-filled Hogtown day, I heard myself telling the Picton real estate guy that if he could find me a short-term rental somewhere, I would jump at it. In short order, a place appeared. The landlord saw me coming—doubled the rent to a sum that only a dumb Torontonian would pay—and soon enough, I was ensconced in a small apartment in a stately home across from the Merrill Inn. My new County bachelor pad had been the home of a woman in her nineties, who was on her way to a care home in Belleville—and it showed in the décor. Lovely flowery window treatments abounded. There was a bedpan stashed away in a closet. The bedroom was a strangely faded rose colour with a wallpaper border to match. Let's just say, it made for an unlikely make-out lair for a gay man on the lookout for love—or whatever. But I refused to be daunted.

When I arrived in the County, I knew a couple people, none close friends. So I was lonely. It was January and I started dating Netflix (I even watched the reboot of *Dynasty*)—and had the occasional tryst with the Regent Movie Theatre. But let's face it: sitting in a movie theatre with seventy grey-haired couples who have been together for thirty years isn't the best place to meet your heart's companion.

After three years of single life, I knew I had to become proactive if I wanted to find a partner for what comes next. So I continued with what I was doing in Toronto to find a new husband: I turned to the dating/sex sites that abound, that connect gay men everywhere. The new gay club where men can meet other men like me with a propensity for showtunes, fastidious fashion, and hot gay random pickups. Except the latter seemed a little impetuous in this community of five thousand, where you tend to bump into people at the Metro or Sandbanks or the Midtown Brewery—suddenly the anonymity of the transaction wasn't quite what it was in the thriving metropolis I had left behind. Even though the SCRUFF profiles featured blurry torso shots of men in relationships, it didn't quite inspire confidence in finding a date for the night—and not a great way to find a husband or even to make a new friend.

But I persisted. And if you buy me a bottle of Long Dog pinot or growler of Parson's Rinda Rinda, I am happy to regale you with a few stories: the sweet-but-oh-so-lonely dog breeder who still essentially lives with his ex; the neurotic artsy type who brings a whole new meaning to the phrase "sex panic"; the handsome husband with whom I had no fewer than five hundred messages back and forth before any kind of hookup; the hot though boring good guy who got unnerved by making out beside the wallpaper patterns in my boudoir—and to be honest, I couldn't blame him—oh, the stories I could tell. You know the perils of online dating: tragedy plus time equals comedy.

It is now early May in the County, and now that it isn't snowing every other day and the snowplows are no longer cementing my car in the driveway, and the ice cream stores are open again, let's just say I have a few prospects. So sorry, Netflix. It's not you, it's me. With spring surging into summer, the possibilities of love and romance seem, well, possible. I am ready to join the human race and look for a fellow who doesn't talk about discretion from the get go. Like Dolly Levi, I'm going to jump back into life and see who I can find for myself in the County, before the parade passes by.

BANK ROBBERY IN WELLINGTON

BY MARY R. LAZIER

In 1935, the Bank of Nova Scotia in Wellington was robbed. A mason named Oscar St. Pierre was hired to build an outside wall when the bank installed a new vault, but he neglected to include cement in the grout. He came back later, dismantled the wall very quietly, so as to not disturb the neighbours, and made off with the vault's contents. Oscar divulged his secret to a friend, who threatened to tell the police unless he was given half the proceeds of the theft. St. Pierre went to the police instead and confessed. The police asked if he still had the money. Oscar replied that he had hidden the stolen coins, amounting to $1,190, in his gas tank, but he didn't know how to get them out. The bank robbery was reported in the *Picton Gazette*, but Oscar's confession to police didn't happen until some months later.

FROM VINYL APRONS TO TAILS AND WHITE GLOVES

BY NIGEL J. SIVEL

Prince Edward County and its people are remarkable in many ways. Back in the 1970s, I discovered a concrete example of this fact far away from my home here in Wellington: I was reminded of the Prince Edward County canning factory in one of Britain's more up-market department stores on Piccadilly Street in the heart of London, England.

Fortnum & Mason (known as just Fortnum's) was founded in 1702 by William Fortnum and Hugh Mason to supply quality food throughout the Victorian era. It has developed into a department store, but still offers exotic, specialty, and basic provisions. The store has opened additional departments, including a gentleman's department on the third floor and its tea shop is well known for the traditional English afternoon tea. The clerks, mostly men, wear formal attire consisting of tails (but no top hats) and white gloves.

One afternoon in the early 1970s, my wife and I were in London spending time with her family and friends. We visited Fortnum's and, just inside the main door, was a pyramid of canned goods each with a large Canadian label. It was pumpkin pie filling. Curious, as pumpkin was rare in Britain then, I went over to the stack under the watchful eye of a clerk or two. Looking at the cans, I discovered that I knew the code number stamped on the top of each can. The code identified the factory where the product had been canned.

Now, I have to back up a bit because not everyone knows about codes on canned goods. My knowledge came from working in the canning factories in Wellington: Greer Brothers Canning Company on Greer street, which is now the location of the Home Hardware Building Centre, and United Canners Limited, owned by Alex Lipson and known locally as Lipson's, that had been located at the corners of Belleville Street and the now-Millennium Trail. The factories processed peas, tomatoes, pumpkins, raspberries, and strawberries, all grown locally.

Mr. Lipson provided lots of work for many people when the factory was in operation, from around 1936 to 1978, when it closed. During our high school days, I worked many summers there with my brother and my mother. We worked the "pea pack" in late June and into July. We remember those days as being long and with time off only for lunch, supper, and coffee breaks—for weeks on end. There was no such thing as a weekend off during "the pack." When the peas were ripe, we had only hours to get them harvested and processed. We arrived around seven a.m. and, for my brother and me, we did not leave until one or two the next morning.

Management seemed to like our work habits, as they trusted us with cleanup at night after the last pea truck and employee had gone home. We spent a couple hours cleaning the factory production areas using large hoses to wash everything down. We were the only two people left on site. Our final job as we left the factory was to lock up—we were entrusted with the keys. It was a short walk home from the factory, and a short sleep before seven a.m. rolled around again.

During the day, my brother worked in the cook room, a hot and steamy place where large cages of canned peas were submerged into boiling vats of water. I worked the machine where peas were graded by running them into a vat of water containing salt and sugar. I had to dump in fifty-pound bags of salt and some sugar to keep the specific gravity at a certain reading. The peas separated themselves according to their weight: the sweeter peas (first grade) were taken off the top. From here the peas went to the sorting tables, slow-moving conveyor belts where numerous hair-netted, vinyl-aproned women, including my mother, sat on each side sorting and chatting for hours on end. The peas were then canned and cooked, with my brother's help, before heading to the labelling warehouse at the back of the building.

And that's how I learned the code numbers I saw stamped on the cans at Fortnum's. The cans were from Mr. Lipson's sister factory in Consecon, where the pumpkin was processed. Little did the formally attired clerks know about the wet, often hot, and sometimes dangerous conditions within the little factory that had produced them, and the hours put in by the high school kids and the many men and women who worked weeks on end during the pack.

I am now in my mid-seventies, and many of my generation raised in the County will remember those factory days. An excellent account of the canning industry in Prince Edward County can be found in Douglas A. Crawford's detailed book, *County Canners: a History of the Canning Industry in Prince Edward County*. Mr. Crawford describes the first factory opening in 1882 through to 1996, when the last cannery closed. At one point, Prince Edward County was the canning capital of Ontario, and perhaps of all of Canada. Today, one name remains: Sprague Foods Limited moved from their Mountain View factory to Belleville in 1996. That was the last canning factory in Prince Edward County. Not a bad run from 1882 to 1996, I would say.

JUST FEELS RIGHT

BY PETA HALL

I was totally fed up with Toronto, the traffic, the pollution, the cost of living, the no-life, the no-community, the constantly working seven days a week. So I decided to get out.

I started searching for a place; I went north to Muskoka, west to Niagara-on-the-Lake, to Georgetown, Merrickville—even the Ottawa Valley. The criteria for moving my clay studio and business was simple. I needed a beautiful place, a good tourist location, and somewhere that just felt right. It took a year of exploring. Finally, early one January, I booked into a beautiful old bed and breakfast set high up on a hill in Brighton. It was the closest accommodation I could find to the County. It was a delightfully faded old farmhouse and all the windows were covered with a thick layer of ice. It was a cold January!

I found a house in Bloomfield, but there was already a potter there. Yikes, what to do? I went to talk to the only store open in the village, an antique shop crammed with treasures. The owner, a very pleasant elderly man, filled me in. He told me about the villagers, the business association (I think he was the chair at the time), the place to find all the news—the post office—or even better, juicier news—the corner store. I knew I had found a new home.

So I moved. I didn't know a soul, didn't know anything about village life, but the place just felt right. I soon met people: a neighbour who remarked, "Well, I saw the blue car stayed overnight last night!"; Johnny Fox on his bike who delivered the papers to the studio door, always with a tidbit of hilarious gossip; the two amazing County men who rescued me after my van hit black ice and careened into a frozen ditch—it was nine-thirty at night and I was just driving back from the airport, still in my African clothing with no boots and no coat!

I learned so much: I learned how to grow a lushly co-lourful garden from my gracious Dutch neighbour, and I learned how my well just kept on pumping, even as my neighbour over the road had to haul in summer water. I learned that you do not dissuade a very large snapping turtle, determinedly emerging from the mill pond and casually walking up your lawn, by using the wooden handle of a rake, because she will promptly bite it off. I learned that if I got up at four-thirty in the morning, I was able to spend glorious, long, peaceful hours gardening before my studio gallery opened at ten. And on those warm, cloudless summer afternoons, I could make it to Lakeshore Lodge by ten after five with a book, wine, and a towel, and swim out into the quiet lake and wonder at just how blessed I was to be there.

I learned about community, about how artists needed to have a voice, show their work, and share why and how they make it: the studio tour was born. I learned that even talented local artists needed a profes-sional show to help the rest of Eastern Ontario discover their creativity: the Maker's Hand was born. I learned we needed a vociferous business association, and our reeve at the time listened and was supportive. I learned that teaching workshops to the community was a truly rewarding, enriching experience. Winter weekends were filled with women who created clay artworks that they still use today!

I met fascinating people who wandered up my gallery stairs, many from away, some wanting not to be and who asked, "Who is a good real estate agent?" or "Where should we eat?"

I learned how to drive the County, to smile and let people cross the street anywhere at any time, to glare and shake a fist at speeding trucks or fancy cars, to happily meander behind tractors laden with bales of hay, to stop for sheep and talk to the herder as they passed. I learned to wave at neighbours with the flick of a hand, and touch my horn to get the attention of a friend who was ignoring me. I learned you can get four cars in front of Bloomfield Post office even though there are only three spaces, and you can even park around the corner, clearly marked POST OFFICE VEHICLES ONLY, if you leave your car running as you pop in to empty your mailbox.

I learned to stop by old-timers on their porches, gentle smoke rising from their ashtrays, and listen to their County stories, the local lore and myths, and gleaned wisdom from these animated conversations. I watched as the colourful hanging baskets were watered with a long hosepipe, connected to a barrel precariously balanced behind a well-loved "tractor." I learned that if you smiled and greeted a villager, they would be happy to natter about the weather, the snowdrifts, the rain or drought, and the best veggies to be found at Van Grootheest.

I learned everyone knew when a new person or family arrived in the village, and you welcomed them as you walked by their home strewn with discarded packing boxes. I learned what a true village community was even though I am from away and will never be County-County as much as I yearn and wish and long for that. But I know I am blessed to be here. It really is home now, after Africa, Europe, Southeast Asia, and various other parts of Canada. Funny how it just feels right.

HEARTBREAK HOTEL

BY PETER AND CELIA SAGE

In early 2007, we learned that the Royal Hotel might be available for sale. Built in 1880-something, it's had many owners and is a real piece of County history. At the time we bought it, it was kind of a dive but quite iconic. The owner lived in the back in his own little apartment and was running it as a rooming house and pool parlour, with entertainment on the weekends, and fights that spilled out into the street. He was in his seventies and had owned it for twenty or thirty years. Over a period of about six months, I met with him frequently to negotiate a sale price. The deal was kind of on again off again because he was hard to pin down, so you had to catch him when he wasn't distracted.

I got together some investors to not only buy the hotel but also to renovate it into a luxury inn and condos. We imagined ten luxury condos and thirty-six guest suites with a restaurant, café, and spa. All of that was encapsulated in this thing.

One of our dreams was that every Thursday night jazz greats Brian Barlow and Guido Basso would host a radio show live from the rooftop lounge of the Royal Hotel. They were up for it. So that became part of the thinking there, to provide a permanent home for the jazz festival performances. We designed an indoor/outdoor jazz lounge. In good weather, you could sit outdoors around a fire pit and listen to live jazz way up on the roof of the Royal. It was quite fun to imagine all of this. Over the next year or so I designed all of the rooms and spaces. It was all three-dimensional, so you could actually go in every room.

We commissioned Harry Farfan, a multi-talented local artist and a real character, to create a model. I think it must have cost five thousand dollars. You could see every brick, every window, everything. Once we commissioned this model and we had a three-dimensional vision of what we had proposed for this thing we finalized the funding for it.

We had funding in place from two different sources to cover both the condo project and the hotel project. We had commitments from two banks and had partners who had put in money. We had most of what we needed—the project was going to cost about fifteen million dollars. All we had left to find was two million dollars more in private equity. We hired a hospitality consultant to help us think about how to market it, how to find people to run it, to get the hospitality industry quotient, and to set up a couple of events to try and get that last equity. We had an event at the Regent Theatre, in what was then called the Cook's Room. We had the model, we had wine and cheese and shmoozy stuff, talking about the project. People got very excited about it. They were reserving their condos, making plans to move into town once it was finished. There was some very real enthusiasm about it.

We also took the Royal Hotel road show to Toronto, to Crush Wine Bar on King Street. We set the model up on a table, and served wine and hors d'oevres. We invited anyone we knew who had a connection to the County, the famous and the almost famous. By the end of the evening we had our two million dollars to go ahead with the project. We celebrated by having dinner at the wine bar.

The next day, the recession hit. Lehman Brothers filed for bankruptcy. We spent the next six months trying to collect the two million dollars pledged that evening. But the project died about a year later.

We tried to find new investors, but the core group that owned it got stuck with the physical building. We were all just trying to keep it from crumbling. Winters came and went, the roof was leaking, and we couldn't sell it. Pigeons were getting in the windows—it was literally falling apart. We'd go up on the roof and there'd be holes that we'd have to tarp over. Finally, we had to turn the power off and basically let the inside of it go.

I think it's important to get this out there, because the word the last few years was that nobody cared about the building, that it was just left to crumble. But the real story is that we were doing everything we could to try to get it to become something, but after a while we couldn't keep up. We didn't have the money to maintain the building, to keep fixing the roof. We just had to close it off so nobody could go in there and get injured. You do your best.

It was a good three or four years before we sold it to Greg Sorbara, who owns it now and has obviously done somewhat what we were envisioning. We're happy to see the Royal coming back to life in the end.

"MAKES NO DIFFERENCE
TO ME -

OR

THE SEEDS"

MORLEY, WRITTEN

BY RONIKA DAYTON

While I do fondly remember my great-grandfather Morley Dayton—his dark sunglasses, white hair, big hands, and the coin he would slip into my hand before I hopped down from his lap—he has taken on a somewhat legendary status in my mind. In part, this is because he died when I was four years old, before I could make too many memories of my own with him, but mostly, it's because he was a blind farmer. I didn't appreciate how impressive that was until relatively recently. To be honest, my granny, Hilda, with her Puritan fashion sense and stern disposition, kind of overshadowed him. Her presence looms large in my memory. But over the years, I've grown more curious about Morley.

The Dayton farm was located in Delhi, which is in Picton. A whole other story could be written about what it was like for my Dad and his siblings growing up in that infamous neighbourhood in the '50s and '60s, but we'll save that for another day. My great-grandparents bought their house, said to be the oldest in Picton, for $3,500. At the same time, they could have bought Macaulay House, and all the way back to the first crossroad, for $7,000, but, according to Dad, "they figured it was a bit much for them to carry, with him being blind." Historically, the house had been known as the White Cottage, and is where newlyweds

Reverend Macaulay and his wife Anne lived while their impressive home was being built on the other side of the street. The house's setting has changed, as the land around it became severed and developed in recent decades, and it doesn't look like much now, but in its prime, the house had five fireplaces and a pastoral setting, with a large barn and frontage onto York Street. My great-grandparents, grandparents, Dad and his six siblings, my grandmother's father, along with at least one of my dad's many cousins, all lived at the farm together, with Granny's sister and her husband (Aunt Vergie and Uncle Clarence) living in a trailer on the property. Other family members lived just up the road. It was always a place where anybody could stop by.

A few years ago, one of my clients told me that she grew up near my great-grandparents' farm, and distinctly remembers Morley's beautiful singing voice. She used to love listening to the sound of his voice drifting through her windows. This surprised me, as I had no idea he was known for his singing. But it makes sense; my dad has always sung, and my brother has one of the most beautiful voices you'll ever hear. I asked Dad about it: "He was out on the farm, singing all the time. He had a really good voice. So many people in the neighbourhood commented on how good his voice was." I wish I could remember it. So I recently pried my dad for more information regarding my great grandfather. I wanted to fill in some blanks and get a better sense of who he was.

Morley was born in Picton in 1907. His parents were George Dayton, born in South Marysburgh in 1864, and Evelena Hineman. He was not born blind, but lost his sight due to diabetes. His eyes were removed. We don't know the exact year that the blindness occurred, but we know it was prior to 1936, as he never saw my grandfather.

Nevertheless, Morley ran the family farm, and tales of his brute strength and abilities abound. He took care of all the animals, milked the cows, raised and killed about seventy-five chickens a year, mended the fences, shingled the house, chopped firewood—whatever needed to be done. A cousin of my father's told me that he once saw my great-grandfather out working late at night, digging away, and when he expressed surprise that Morley was out so late working in the pitch dark, Morley replied, "Makes no difference to me!"

He worked at the sales barn, loading up the cattle and pigs. He worked in canning factories in East Lake, taking boxes of tomatoes off the line and stacking them onto pallets. Harold Fawcett put a few stakes in the ground and tied a rope between them, and Morley dug the main water line in Fawcettville by hand with a pickaxe and shovel, following the rope. And nobody could beat him in an arm wrestle.

In any season, Morley would open up the barn door, start the car, and drive it out so it was ready to go for Granny, who cleaned other peoples' houses. From time to time, Morley's friends picked him up and took him out on a horn trip. Once they got out far enough, they would get a kick out of putting him behind the wheel.

Morley often cooked meals for my dad, who loved his cooking, and my dad would take his grandfather uptown every other week for a haircut at Sibthorpe's. Afterwards, they would go for ice cream at Teasel's Drug Store, or to the Chinese restaurant beside the theatre.

Morley, who would make time for anyone, was well-known, and well-liked. People walking or driving by the farm would say, "Hello, Morley," and he would greet them back by name. To my mom, who started dating my dad when they were teenagers at Prince Edward Collegiate Institute, he was a gentle giant. My dad says that he never heard him say an angry word. I am proud to say that I am the great-granddaughter of a true County gem.

CARVING THE VINEYARD

BY RYAN MONKMAN

In the County, grapevines are tied to the ground and then covered in soil to protect them from our harsh winter. Any part of the vine left above ground can freeze to death. The buried vines stay cozy and dream of spring, when it's time to dehill.

Dehilling is delicate: a dance of shaving soil, loosening, and lifting. If you're too gentle, the vine stays buried. If you're too aggressive, you break the vine. Each farm has its own melody, but there's a common rhythm.

Begin with a mound of soil two feet wide, two feet deep, and hundreds of feet long. Somewhere inside there's a tangled web of vine and wire. Steel T-bars reach skyward every eight plants.

Shave the hill. A plow scrapes the side of each mound. A tractor pulls the trimmed soil away. The farmer pushes herself forward. Each pass of the tractor cuts the mound a little deeper. Every inch trimmed increases the vine's chance of survival. Too deep and the vine is ripped from the earth.

The farmer sits in her cab for days. Alone. She's focused on the ground beneath her. Her thoughts wander to the season ahead and the life she shares with these vines.

Next, she greets the soil with a grape hoe—a dull blade on a hydraulic swinging arm. Whack. Whack.

The hoe slams against the hill, loosing and crumbling. The farmer senses where each vine sits, then cracks the soil in between. She balances gentleness and aggression. She counts off the vines; eight per T-bar. She knows her field.

The farmer sees her vines take shape after months underground. She remembers the smell of new growth. The sweetness of harvest. The cool nights spent walking her rows.

And then she goes in on foot. She knocks any remaining soil loose. She crouches next to the vine. She places her pruners against the low wire and cuts the vine free, releasing the vine into the sun.

Soft rain will clean the plant. Another pass with the tractor will smooth any sign that the hill was ever there. The vines are ready. The earth is awake.

ABSINTHE ON EAST LAKE

BY SARAH WILLIAMS

From the days of rum-running to our current wine and beer-soaked palates, Prince Edward County has been a purveyor of not only libation, but also adventure. I was sixteen when I became aware of the tempestuous relationship these two things have in our community, where Lake Ontario snaps around our periphery like a rubber band.

My brother had just moved home to stay with my parents for a year. We lived in an ancestral mausoleum—a house steeped in stories told and untold. We had several ancient maples in the yard, and a back porch shaded from the sun and neighbours alike. It was there that my brother set up his still. It stood handsomely as he toiled every weekend on new recipes for liqueurs, essences, or even absinthe.

At this time, I was so close to being a child that I still spent most of my time observing others, as children aren't invited into the adult world for the most part. But my brother was different. And when I was sixteen, he took me to a friend's party on East Lake Road. It was my first party and the first time I'd ever had a drink.

We poured into his tiny car and set off down an old farmer's road, tall grass pushing through the windows. When we got there, the sun had begun to set. There was live music in the barn, camaraderie, and fire. And when the sun went down, my brother brought out his absinthe, stored in unassuming mason jars. Van Morrison's "Moon Dance" started playing on a nearby radio, crickets chirped, and the sound of the crackling fire mingled with laughter up into the night sky.

That night was just one strand in a web of magic that lies across this land. It brings us together, often around fire and libation. Prince Edward County has the peculiar ability to make time stand still. Perhaps it is because there are still shorelines to walk and people to listen. It is like a lull in the universe. It is our community.

THE ONE-MAN PARTY

BY STARKS

One thing we did for fun was pile in a car and crawl along the back roads. The point wasn't to go anywhere or do anything in particular except drive around and smoke bongs.

These were those carefree and careless days when we had nothing better to do than melt a fresh bottle in the oven, pop a stem and bowl in it, kit up with a sesh tray and scissors, a few g's, and hit the road.

People of a certain generation will remember the classic County pull-through bong. There was a basic design that was popular with pretty much everyone, though everyone had their own style of making them. Basically, it was a plastic pop bottle that you heated up in the oven so that it made a specific shape. You used a second bottle to make the mouthpiece and taped it together.

There was a particular art to getting the stem in there with a perfect seal. If you could get to a head shop, you used a manufactured stem and bowl. Failing that, you used what you could find. I'm willing to bet half the dads in the County couldn't figure out why they could never find their ten millimetre sockets; a thumbhole in the back for a carb and you're good to go.

Anyhow, this time, we took the long way. Picked up the other Dave and the One-Man Party in Wellington, cruised through West Lake, the twisty way through the dunes and Sandbanks. Picked up Mike on the other side of East Lake. Dave was driving his old Civic and the One-Man Party was sitting shotgun. I was riding in the back with the other Dave and Mike. We backtracked up the forty-foot hill and parked at the end to dip our toes.

All along, we listened to tunes: Rage Against the Machine, Cypress Hill, Wu-Tang, Nirvana, Pearl Jam, mix tapes. We told stories and cracked jokes and generally talked shit. The kinds of things that are at once forgettable and memorable.

We piled back in the car and were raising dust.

Out of nowhere, and in the middle of it too, the One-Man Party started laughing (or maybe he'd never stopped) and in his way of perpetual amusement and excitement, he told Dave to stop the car.

"Stop! Stop!"

We were on a dirt road, no houses in sight, no cars, not even any cows.

Dave stopped. The One-Man Party unfolded himself out of the small Civic, jogged around the front of the car, and climbed down into the roadside ditch.

The rest of us looked at each other and at the One-Man Party like, "What the fuck?"

Down there in the ditch, he seemed to be taking his pants off. He *did* take his pants off. And then he put them back on. All the while laughing hysterically to himself.

None of us had any idea what he was up to, but that's kind of why we call him the One-Man Party—he's always got a big smile on his face. It's never a boring time when he's around, and not because he's just trying to win everyone's approval. Maybe there's a bit of that mixed in, but he's just a genuine comedian, a guy who goes through life making himself and everyone around him laugh.

The One-Man-Party scrambled up from the ditch with his tighty-whities in his hand and squatted down in front of the car, his back to us.

At this point we were equal parts mystified and amused.

After a minute he jogged back to the car, folded himself in, and told Dave: "Go! Go!"

So Dave went.

We laughed our heads off.

The One-Man Party had carefully lain his gitch in the middle of the road, and placed some small rocks along the edges so it wouldn't blow away.

We asked him why he'd done it, and he said that he'd just been thinking that it would be hilarious if we were driving along and came across someone's underwear put out on the road like that.

So he'd done it for the next guy.

And that's basically a day in the life of some high school kids in Prince Edward County in the late 1990s. Someone had a car, someone had a bong, someone had some weed, and everyone had time to kill.

COUNTY KINDNESS

BY TARA WILKINSON

My husband and I moved to the County from Toronto with our energetic four-year-old daughter in early December 2007. It was the start of what would become the worst winter we've encountered in our eleven years since as full-time residents. By the Family Day long weekend in February, I was really starting to suffer from cabin fever; soft snow was falling and I desperately needed to get out of the house for some time on my own. I told my husband I was heading out for a while to shoot photographs of the County. He told me to drive carefully, and I bundled up and headed out with my camera at the ready on the seat beside me.

Down around Sandbanks, I spotted some wild turkeys grazing in a field of snow-covered corn. The side of the road looked like it had just been plowed smooth, so I pulled over—and my Jeep suddenly tipped to the right and sank deep into the ditch.

Several attempts to move the Jeep back and forth only made things worse. I managed to get myself out by climbing out the driver-side door. The snow was now heavy and wet as I walked to the nearest farmhouse to get help. There was no answer at the first one. I pounded on the door of the next house. I heard a deep, loud, frightening, "WOOOOOOOOF!" and freaked out as a large Great Dane approached the window.

I turned and started to hightail it down the driveway when I heard a voice shout at me from behind. "Everything okay? Do you need any help?" An older gentleman stood in the doorway with his arm resting on the top of his enormous dog's head. I soon learned it was Clifford Foster, patriarch of one of the County's long-standing and successful farm families.

Without approaching, I shouted my woeful tale of what had happened and asked if he might have some farm equipment that could pull my vehicle out. "Oh, my son's just gone down to Milford with the tractor, and I don't know when he'll be back. Let me come take a look."

He grabbed his coat and invited me to jump into his handy-dandy snow-chomping golf cart. Off we drove to the site of my sad situation. He got out, walked around to look at the front of the Jeep and declared: "Why, you got her in there *good*."

Realizing he likely couldn't help me without the tractor, I said, I'd just call CAA and see how long it would take for them to come out. I expected them to be very busy on a day like this and the wait would likely be long.

Clifford said, "Well, you're not going to wait out here in this weather. Come on back to the house to keep warm and have a cup of tea."

He must have sensed my hesitation or noticed the look of terror in my eyes. I said, "I have to admit … I'm terrified of that dog you have." Clifford replied "Oh, him? He won't hurt you. If anything, he'll just lick you to death."

Wondering what I'd gotten myself into, off we went back to his place. After I placed the call to CAA, I sat in a chair near the kitchen table as Clifford put the kettle on.

My entire body froze as the Great Dane approached me. As promised, he slurped up the side of my face, then turned himself around and backed his behind onto my lap, sitting on me with all four paws still on the ground.

I laugh remembering this moment. When it happened, not so much.

On Clifford's kitchen table, there was a pile of odd-looking equipment. I asked what it was for.

He explained that he was making sugar maple candies, and that they produce syrup every spring from the thousands of maple trees on their farm. He then mentioned that the Maple in the County festival was coming up, and they needed to get some new labels made for their syrup bottles.

"We can help you with that," I said. He looked at me and said "Really?" I explained that my husband and I ran a successful design studio called Fire Engine, and that producing a new label for him would be the least we could do to thank him for his kindness and generosity.

About six weeks later, the new label was launched, and it's been featured on his Fosterholm syrup bottles ever since. From that gloomy winter's day forward, Clifford and I have been friends. He continues to delight in introducing me as the woman he met in a ditch.

Over the years since that day, we have at times come home to find pumpkins or apples left on our porch steps, dropped off by Clifford on his way home from selling at the farmer's market in Belleville. At other times, he's backed his truck down the driveway, thrown open the back door and asked, "What do you need?"

Clifford's kindness and friendship has meant a lot to us. He's taught us the true meaning of "help thy neighbour"—and that by living in the County, we are all part of a community that looks out for one another.

FULL MOON BAY

BY VICKI EMLAW

When I was a kid, my sisters, cousins, and I basically lived at my grandma's cottage every summer.

She grew up in a big old house next to a big old barn that says Hicks Holme on it, right next to Little Bluff—that's the land that my family settled when they came to North America. After she and my grandfather got married, they moved to Milford, but they built a cottage down the hill from her family home. My grandmother's brother lived in the house on the hill. He was a farmer named Rex Hicks.

I told this story at my grandmother's funeral; it's a story about myself and my sisters and my mother and my aunts and my grandmother. On this particular day, I was nine or ten years old. There was a huge storm, what my grandmother called a nor'easter, which always meant huge wind and huge waves. Half Moon Bay is open water coming from the east, so when the wind comes in from the northeast it always makes gigantic waves. We used to love going swimming in the nor'easters because of that.

I'm not sure if my sister Becky was old enough, so it must have been my sister Aynsley, my cousin Christine, and I think her mom was there, and my mom, a couple of other women, and my grandmother. We had all decided we were going to go out swimming. Well, *we* didn't decide: my grandmother decided, and when she decided something it meant everybody was taking part. She turned everything into a party, so everybody wanted to do it anyway. Grandma loved being naked, so she decided we were all going skinny-dipping. We were the only ones around and the waves were huge and we were so excited about going out into the waves.

All of the water for my great-uncle Rex's farm—for the animals, the crops—all of it came from the bay, from a pipe that went down the hill and into the water. And the waves were so big that day they broke the pipe apart. Rex didn't have any water up the hill, so he came down to see what the problem was. He was probably about five hundred or so feet over to the east of where we were swimming.

Rex got in the water to try to fix the pipe.

All of a sudden, we heard a man yelling at us from near the shore. Because the waves were so big, they were really loud, so we couldn't make out what he was saying—and we didn't want a man to see us naked, so we all started screaming too, which made it even harder to hear him.

A huge wave had splashed over him and knocked his glasses off, so he couldn't see anything at all. He couldn't see who was in the water, and he couldn't yell loud enough to get our attention to get us out of the water to help him or tell us what was happening. He was freaking out because we were freaking out. He couldn't see and we couldn't hear. Everything went around in circles and around in circles.

It was my grandma who finally waded out of the water, wrapped herself in a towel, and decided to go see what was happening. I'm grateful to be like my grandmother, in the way of collecting people to do things together and creating a party out of any old activity—you just have to look at it from a different perspective. And also: the freedom to feel okay with yourself and wanting to not wear clothes and be free and have fun in the water, in nature.

WAUPOOS WEDDING

BY DOMENICO CAPILONGO

at the winery
in the vineyard

roses, red sentinels
are upstaged by the bride

the groom aglow on the dock
not waiting but wanting

three generations take in the evening
with a collective sigh

one slow kiss
seals the entire day

reminding us
how easy love really is

CONTRIBUTOR BIOGRAPHIES

Domenico Capilongo is a high-school creative writing teacher and karate instructor. His first books of poetry, *I thought elvis was italian, hold the note*, and short fiction collection, *Subtitles*, almost won several awards. His latest book of poetry, *send*, is about the way we communicate. His new manuscript is based on the song "Salt Peanuts."

Born a Montrealer, **Alan Gratias** is a Waupoosian at heart and flies the flag of North Maryburgh where he lives. He restores crumbling houses and profiles singular people. He created the Gravitas brand in the belief that we are all on a quest for authenticity and connection. When he is not writing about detective dogs and everyday wisdom, he tends to ongoing deterioration.

Alex Schultz has been an acquiring editor of fiction and nonfiction at Penguin Canada and HarperCollins Canada and for many years was a senior acquiring editor of nonfiction at McClelland & Stewart. He grew up by the sea in Ireland and lives and works in Picton.

Alysa Hawkins moved to the County with her husband and three children in 2013. She had always been a good student but never thought she would move into a school full time. She enjoys painting, raising chickens, and writing when she is not running her seasonal bed and breakfast, South in Milford.

Anne Preston lives on a hobby farm in the County. She has worked at Books & Company, with the County Reads and County Kids Read programs, and the Al Purdy A-Frame project. Anne is a member of Writers Unblocked, a memoir group of talented women.

Astrid Young is a singer-songwriter, writer, and sommelier. Her written work includes several screenplays and the best-selling chronicle of her life growing up in an iconic Canadian family, *Being Young: Scott, Neil and Me*. Born and raised in Toronto, her career has taken her around the world. She now makes Picton her home.

Becky Mulridge is only a third-generation County person— so is that even bonafide? She works at Books & Company through the week and sings with the band Cue the Funk on weekends. In between, she shares farm life with her husband, Chris, three children, two cats, one dog and many pretty chickens.

Shortly after submitting his essay for this anthology, **Benjamin Carter Thornton** came to his senses and relocated to Prince Edward County. He now lives in Picton with his wife and three children, where he works as a real estate agent. He rarely finds himself far from Glenwood Cemetery.

Brian L. Flack has published three novels and a collection of poems. He has contributed literary and social criticism to books, periodicals, academic journals, and newspapers, and hosted the radio program "Bookviews" on Q-107 in Toronto. For almost forty years, he was a professor of English Literature.

Buffy Carruthers worked in Toronto as a freelance journalist for the *Globe & Mail* and Maclean Hunter small press. She began writing fiction in PEC in the early 1990s and has a story in *The County Wave* (Cressy Lakeside). She is currently working on a collection of short stories. As a visual artist, she shows at Blizzmax and Maison Depoivre galleries.

Carolyn Barnes is a retired librarian and lifelong devotee of the written word. She and her husband fell in love with the County in the late 1980s, finally making it their full-time home in 2005. After twelve happy years, they followed family to the Okanagan, another magical part of the world.

J.D. Carpenter is the author of five novels (the Campbell Young Mysteries and, most recently, *The County Murders*) and four books of poetry. He lives in Prince Edward County.

Cheryl Bruce is a classical clarinetist and educator. She lives in Prince Edward County.

Christian Webber's life has taken him from coast to coast. His work started at school in British Columbia, where he received a diploma in journalism and photojournalism from the Western Academy of Photography. After years on the

West Coast, the prairies, and Toronto, he is settled back in Nova Scotia where he lives and writes alone.

Christine Renaud is an artmaker, community organizer, and anarchist living on Haudenosaunee, Huron-Wendat, and Mohawk land in Prince Edward County. When she's not challenging the status quo, you'll find her lost in a good book or playing a board game. And she'll likely be on her third cup of coffee.

Debbie Hyatt moved home to PEC six years ago. She resides in Bloomfield with her happy dog and her mild cat and goes by the name Ava Darling. Having been away for forty years, she experiences herself living in an interesting grey zone between the old and the new.

Deborah Troop has been happily living in Prince Edward County for nearly eight years. She volunteers at Picton Memorial Hospital, spends the long Canadian winters writing stories, and is a member of the group Writers Unblocked. Her memoir, *My First Wedding*, is available at Amazon.ca.

Gabriele Cole studied Art History and Curatorial Studies at York University. After working at some of the top cultural institutions in Toronto, Gabriele chose to move back to her home in Prince Edward County. She currently lives in an 89 square-foot tiny house, surrounded by gardens, writing short essays.

Gerry Jenkison is a visual artist living in Hillier, where she and her husband Don raise organic chickens and grow hops on their small farm. Her love of nature and animals extends to being a field naturalist, including the preservation of trees in the County.

Helen Williams became a part of a Bloomfield farming family when she moved to Prince Edward County from Perth County in 1959. Gardening, operating Wilhome Farmhouse B & B, leading 4-H, working with Welcome Wagon and writing memoirs have been interspersed with raising four children with her husband Bob. Now there are grandchildren and great-grandchildren to enjoy.

Hilary Arthur Amolins is a writer, property host, and County FM volunteer. He recently published *Alphabet Animals*, a collection of life lessons for children and young adults. Hilary works and plays in the County.

Jack Evans was born in 1935 and grew up in Belleville. He was a journalist for sixty years on radio and in print media, and continues as a freelance writer in retirement. Married to Nancy Hall, he has a son and three daughters, two surviving. Jack sings in a choir and barbershop group and is an amateur actor.

Jane Moon is fortunate to call herself a County girl who had the sense to return after a number of years away. She resides in her family home with her dog Molly and two cats.

Janet Kellough is the author of seven Thaddeus Lewis mysteries. She has also written two contemporary novels, a speculative fiction thriller, and the semi-non-fictional *Legendary Guide to Prince Edward County*. She lives in an unfashionable part of North Marysburgh.

Karen Palmer is the author of *Spellbound: Inside West Africa's Witch Camps*. Her journalism work has appeared in the *Toronto Star, Washington Times, Sydney Morning Herald,* and *South China Morning Post*, while her fictional work has appeared in the *Dalhousie Review*.

Kimball Lacey's winemaking journey started in 2003 with the first planting of vines and has blossomed into a ten-acre vineyard and winery. His focus is on producing premium award-winning small batch wines with character. Lacey Estates opened its doors to the public in 2009.

Laurie Scott is a retired teacher who was born and raised in Prince Edward County. In 2017, she teamed up with Cressy Lakeside Books and published her debut novel, *In Like a Lion*. A second in this crime series will be released later this year.

Krista Dalby is the Artistic Director of The Department of Illumination, producing magical art events such ICE BOX and The Firelight Lantern Festival. She lives on Clarke Road and is a neighbour to **Loris Wager**.

Louise Bazett-Jones is a teacher and writer who lives on a farm in North Marysburgh with her husband, a chocolate lab, and twenty chickens. She is involved in efforts to improve food security through community building.

Rev. Lynne Donovan came to the County in 2007 to serve St. Andrew's Presbyterian Church in Picton.

At her home on the Bay of Quinte, **Marion Casson** works in paint and fibre. Weaving on a floor loom, working wool fibres into felt, creating scarves and wearables and painting in acrylics. The walls of her house are the exhibition space for paintings and wall pieces.

Max Souliere grew up in Sault Ste. Marie. He retired from the CBC Toronto in 2016 and relocated to Picton with his lovely wife Donna Young. This is Max's first real attempt at writing.

Michael Solberg Schellenberg lives outside Milford.

Mary Lazier's family arrived in Prince Edward County in 1791, following the American Revolution. Her early relatives were George I. Lazier and Alcina Hart, founders of Hart-Lazier pottery. Mary has been making pottery since 1972, and has written and illustrated five heritage books.

Nigel J. Sivel was born in Picton and taught English and Media Literacy at Prince Edward Collegiate Institute from 1971 to 2000. He is a co-founder (with Susan Sivel and Larry Tayler) of the Regent Theatre Foundation and Quinte Summer Music, and a past member of the board for Prince Edward-Hastings Habitat for Humanity.

Peta Hall has been an arts activist all her life, working to promote the arts into everyday living whether in Canada, Hong Kong, or Africa.

Peter Sage's relationship with the County's built heritage preceded his marriage to **Celia** by just a few years, and there hasn't been a dull moment since. Originally from Oshawa, Peter has been building walls in the County since the 1980s and Celia has been making paintings to hang on them.

Ronika Dayton loves planning trips, taking pictures, planting flowers, and going to the beach. She is currently hard at work raising the next generation of County boys.

Ryan (and Nicole) **Monkman** (with help from a toddler and newborn) run FieldBird Cider. The Monkmans follow biodynamics on their farms. When not at FieldBird, Ryan is a production consultant with a focus on emergent technology and oak.

Sarah Williams lives in Picton with her dog and her boyfriend. Having grown up in Prince Edward County, she recently returned home, where the geography and people continue to inspire her writing.

Starks moved from Toronto to Prince Edward County in the 1990s and finished high school at PECI. He lives in Picton with his wife and their two young children.

Tara Wilkinson is an award-winning photographer and fibre artist. She and her husband Andrew are the artist-owners of the new contemporary ANDARA Gallery, whimsical Love Nest Gallery, and rustic Andrew Csafordi Gallery—all located on their beautiful farm at 54 Wilson Road, northwest of Bloomfield.

Vicki Emlaw is an eighth-generation farmer from South Bay. She started Vicki's Veggies back in 2001 and continues the family tradition to this day. When she isn't growing her famous tomatoes, she teaches yoga at Vicki's Yoga and promotes healthy living in PEC.

EDITOR & ILLUSTRATOR BIOGRAPHIES

Tanya Finestone has called the County home for close to twenty years. She has always loved books and works for Invisible Publishing, where she gets to help make them.

Leigh Nash runs Invisible Publishing, which landed in Picton in 2016 by way of Marmora, Montreal, Halifax, and Toronto. She is the author of *Goodbye, Ukulele*, and in addition to making books, she is also a tarot card reader and yoga teacher.

Nella Casson is Prince Edward County born and raised. She completed the art and art history BFA and diploma program through the University of Toronto/Sheridan College. She lives in a brick triplex from 1910 in the heart of Picton, where she balances art and work along with various illustrative projects for the local community of entrepreneurs and dreamers.

ACKNOWLEDGEMENTS

Many people contributed their time and energy to get this book out into the world. A huge pile of thank yous to David Sweet for helping nurture our seedling of an idea and inspiring us with tales of Miss Pickles. To Becky Mulridge, our sounding board on all things Prince Edward County and officemate extraordinaire. Isabelle Patton designs the best windows and is always willing to help with anything. Books & Company in general for treating us like family. Nathan Shubert tracked down some stories that would otherwise have gone unheard. Andrew Faulkner, for lending us his eagle eyes and bringing cinnamon buns when we needed them most. And to Koa, Mallee, Martha—the next generation of County kids—we can't wait to hear your stories one day. Lastly, the biggest thank you of all to everyone who took the time to spread the word about this project, and everyone who took the time to submit.

Royalties from sales of *Don't Honk Twice* will benefit the Prince Edward Learning Centre, an organization dedicated to helping adult learners acquire skills to achieve their personal learning and employment goals.

INVISIBLE PUBLISHING produces fine Canadian literature for those who enjoy such things. As an independent, not-for-profit publisher, our work includes building communities that sustain and encourage engaging, literary, and current writing.

Invisible Publishing has been in operation for over a decade. We released our first fiction titles in the spring of 2007, and our catalogue has come to include works of graphic fiction and nonfiction, pop culture biographies, experimental poetry, and prose.

We are committed to publishing diverse voices and experiences. In acknowledging historical and systemic barriers, and the limits of our existing catalogue, we strongly encourage LGBTQ2SIA+, Indigenous, and writers of colour to submit their work.

Invisible Publishing is also home to the Bibliophonic series of music books and the Throwback series of CanLit reissues.

If you'd like to know more please get in touch:
info@invisiblepublishing.com

Invisible